MICHAEL RAMSEY

The
Anglican
Spirit

Dale
EDITOR

COWLEY PUBLICATIONS
Cambridge, Massachusetts

© 1991 Estate of Michael Ramsey

Published in the United States of America by Cowley Publications, a division of the Society of St. John the Evangelist. No portion of this book may be reproduced, stored in or introduced into a retrieval system, or transmitted, in any form or by any means—including photocopying—without the prior written permission of Cowley Publications, except in the case of brief quotations embodied in critical articles and reviews.

International Standard Book Number: 1-56101-027-8
Library of Congress Number: 91-6599

Library of Congress Cataloging-in-Publication Data
Ramsey, Michael, 1904 - 1988
  The Anglican spirit / Michael Ramsey : Dale Coleman, editor.
    p. cm.
  Includes index.
  ISBN 1-56101-027-8
  1. Anglican Communion—History. 2. Anglican Communion—Doctrines.
3. Anglican Communion—Relations—Catholic Church. 4. Anglican Communion—Relations—Anglican Communion. 6. Orthodox Church—Relations—Anglican Communion. I. Coleman, Dale, 1951 - . II. Title.
BX5005.R35 1991
283—dc20   91-6599

This book is printed on acid-free paper and was produced in the United States of America.

Cowley Publications
28 Temple Place
Boston, Massachusetts 02111

Acknowledgments

I WOULD LIKE TO acknowledge first of all the gracious approval Lady Ramsey gave to this project following her husband's death in April, 1988, along with the very generous assistance given me by Bishop Ramsey's literary executor, John Miles, formerly the Archbishop's press secretary and now Chief Press and Public Affairs Officer for the General Synod of the Church of England. I also wish to thank Nashotah House for providing a haven for the Ramseys in their retirement, a seminary for training Episcopal priests in the Anglo-Catholic tradition which Bishop Ramsey loved.

I am grateful to Mary Puhl, Pam Cabaniss, and especially to Peggy Worzalla for transcribing these lectures and making changes in successive drafts. Here I must also mention my thanks to the parish community of St. Thomas of Canterbury Church, Greendale, Wisconsin, for allowing me to do this work while serving them as their rector. Roger J. White, Charles Gaskell, James Griffiss, Louis Weil, and Wayne L. Smith all gave me valuable assistance in locating certain references.

Cynthia Shattuck, my editor, has edited the transcripts of Bishop Ramsey's lectures for publication and made innumerable helpful suggestions that have strengthened the book. Her continuing support for this project has been most gratifying to me.

Finally, I wish to express my deep gratitude to two women who have taught me more about real Christian love than I can convey in a few words. At various times over the past eight years, my mother, Major Eva Coleman, and my wife, Susan, have encouraged me to continue the work on this book for the same reasons I have desired its publication: their love for Jesus Christ and his church, and their love for Michael Ramsey. This book is dedicated to them.

Dale D. Coleman
Pentecost 1990

Table of Contents

Foreword

A Portrait of Michael Ramsey

Arthur Michael Ramsey was born in 1904, the son of a Congregationalist father, who was also a Cambridge mathematician, and an Anglican mother. The university and the church figured heavily not only in his family background, but also in his own life, although for awhile it seemed that politics would hold sway in his life. Ramsey was elected President of the Cambridge Union while still an undergraduate, a sure sign of future success for the budding Liberal politician—even if, by the 1920s, the party's best years were behind it. By the end of the same year of his election to the Union's presidency in 1926, however, and after much soul-searching, Ramsey decided to pursue holy orders in the Church of England.

The reasons for this decision were complex, but they surely included his discovery of Anglo-Catholic worship while at Cambridge. Among the many priests who influenced him was Conrad Noel, to whose beautiful parish church at Thaxted in northwest Essex Ramsey and a few other students bicycled on Sundays. Noel was famous as an Anglo-Catholic socialist who was a follower of F. D. Maurice's Christian Socialism and Stewart Headlam's Socialist Guild of St. Matthew. Ramsey would always be interested in social and political questions, and his Anglo-Catholicism was never a form of escapism for him. He had also been influenced by the writings of William Temple and Charles Gore (both are given separate chapters by Ramsey here). But for whatever reasons, it soon became obvious to Ramsey that it was not socio-political and economic solutions that would save the world, but Jesus Christ; only theology, not law or politics, would grasp him deeply enough to give his life to its study and thought.

Looking back, Ramsey's career may appear to have been a smooth, steady ascent from lecturer at Lincoln and professor at Durham and Cambridge Universities; to becoming bishop of Durham, one of a handful of really prominent sees in England, at the relatively young age of forty-eight; to his subsequent translations to the archbishoprics of York and, finally, Canterbury in 1961. But this picture misses two key points about Ramsey. One has to do with the personal struggles he went through in his early years as the younger brother of an important philosopher, Frank P. Ramsey, who, while only two years older than he, was light years ahead in terms of intellectual brilliance. Furthermore, his brother was an atheist. In his teens Frank had become known as an extremely gifted mathematician who worked closely with Ludwig Wittgenstein; the latter credited Ramsey with helping him change the direction of his early work, and with bringing him back to Cambridge in the late 1920s. Michael looked up to his older brother as the brightest man he knew, so their continuous and rankling arguments over the existence of God and the metaphysics of Christianity discomforted him greatly. Only with much determination did he decide to enter seminary. Frank's tragic death in 1930 at the age of twenty-seven was not only a terrible loss both to his family and to the world of philosophy—John Maynard

Keynes, Bertrand Russell, A. J. Ayer, and of course Wittgenstein.

However, the death of his brother was presaged by an even greater loss in 1927 just as Ramsey had entered Cuddesdon, a theological seminary near Oxford. His mother was killed in an automobile accident in which his father had been driving. Once again it was with a great effort of will that Ramsey decided to proceed with his priestly formation, but not until after he had taken a leave of absence that included regular visits to a psychologist in London in order to deal with the very severe depression that followed. Ever after he was unable to speak of his mother without great emotion, and he refused to drive an automobile. Ramsey did, when asked, recommend the still fairly young discipline of psychotherapy as treatment for those who suffered, as he had, from depression.

The second point that must be made about Ramsey is this: he was very happy as an academic theologian. His biographer, Owen Chadwick, writes that Ramsey had no aspirations to becoming a bishop and considered his vocation to be that of a New Testament scholar in the service of Jesus Christ and the church.[1] One of his most remarkable qualities was his humility, which so many have identified as saintliness. Some may have guessed that Ramsey had it in him to be a fine scholar-bishop like Butler, Westcott, or Henson; but who could have known that he would much later be compared with a mere handful of Archbishops of Canterbury who have stood out among all the others? Perhaps even a century or so from now Michael Ramsey will routinely be compared with two giants among the Archbishops of Canterbury in the past half-millennium, Thomas Cranmer and Matthew Parker, both of the sixteenth century, a time as turbulent and confusing as this half of the twentieth.

The first time I recall hearing about Archbishop Ramsey was in 1965 after my parents, who were Salvation Army officers, returned from their first trip abroad to attend the Salvation Army's Centenary celebration in England. For these midwesterners, the entire month-long pilgrimage to the land of General William Booth, John Wesley, and William Shakespeare (in that order) was a tremendously joyful time, highlighted by a huge rally of Salvationists at the Royal Albert Hall with the Archbishop of Canterbury as keynote preacher. At the age of eleven, I was struck by their enthusiasm as they pointed to a small figure in the middle of the picture projected on the screen, as well as by the exotic title of this official of the Church of England.

Years later, when I decided to become an Episcopalian, I was given a couple of books of Michael Ramsey's by a very wise and discerning priest, Fr. Wayne Smith, who also made sure that I heard Ramsey preach at the Roman Catholic cathedral in Milwaukee. Both the sermon and the books, in particular *The Gospel and the Catholic Church*, were crucial to my own theological development and spiritual formation. I had thought that John A. T. Robinson's *Honest to God* and then Paul Tillich's theology would satisfy one who had found the extreme conservative Evangelicalism of the church of his youth too constricting, but spirituality, the importance of the church and the sacraments, as well as the need to believe in Jesus Christ as Lord and Savior, were all missing from their Christianity. In Ramsey's work I discovered an expression of the faith that could challenge and sustain me. Bernard M. G. Reardon summarizing F. D. Maurice's doctrine says exactly what I believe to be true about Michael Ramsey's theology:

Orthodox religion, and Anglicanism in particular, has seldom been served by a body of ideas so consistently recognizable as the utterance of a mind profoundly Christian in all its convictions.[2]

I first met Bishop Ramsey in the late fall of my first year at Nashotah House Seminary in 1977. This Anglo-Catholic Episcopal seminary in southeast Wisconsin had become the favorite retreat for the Ramseys and one they visited for extended periods during two of the three years I studied there. At such a small school it was relatively easy to become acquainted with the bishop—easy, that is, if you wanted to engage him on a serious subject and not expect him to spend time in the "small talk" of which he was notoriously intolerant. Ramsey would also lapse into frequent "yes, yes, yes, yesses"—someone once counted twenty-two in a row during a conversation—or begin humming old Victorian hymns in the midst of a discussion. He disliked the attempt by some students to "totemize" him by requesting his opinion on some controversial matter facing the church—the students would then use his answer to cap all further talk on the subject at lunchtime.

In the Nashotah House library I built up enough courage to walk over to the Bishop and inform him that I spent nearly two years reading Paul Tillich. "Don't you think that's enough?" was his impatient reply. I tried again by raising the subject of Anglican theologians of the late nineteenth-century, and scored a direct hit. Ramsey, after all, had written *From Gore to Temple,* a superb account of Anglican theology from 1889, when Charles Gore edited *Lux Mundi*—an epochal work by Liberal Catholics in the Church of England—to William Temple's death in 1944. What did the Bishop think of the view that he himself was the end of a rich line of Anglican theologians extending back through the *Lux Mundi* school to Maurice and some of the Tractarians to Bishop Butler and even beyond? Ramsey "yes, yessed" for awhile and responded by first acknowledging the compliment, then after a long sigh noting the poor shape of present Anglican theology.

I came away impressed from this first of many meetings with the force of his personality. Ramsey was a deeply spiritual man who enjoyed thinking and questioning and intense argument. I was equally impressed by the breadth of his mind, for he enjoyed talking politics immensely, present and past. On one occasion, I admitted that my favorite English politician in the past was Lord Randolph Churchill, Winston Churchill's father. Ramsey "yes, yes, yessed," then launched into a long recitation of Churchill's famous "Chips" speech, which had been a devastating political attack on another of Ramsey's heroes, William Gladstone. Ramsey then analyzed a number of political leaders, beginning with Winston Churchill (who had nominated Ramsey to the Durham See in 1952), Hugh Gaitskell, Harold Wilson, and Edward Heath; he had an uncanny ability to imitate their voices and mannerisms.

American political leaders he tended to disparage, except for Adlai Stevenson, which I put down to a form of English superiority towards Americans typical of many of his class and generation. I remember defensively retorting on this occasion that without American political leaders like Roosevelt, Britain would now be a fifth-rate satellite country speaking German. He quietly informed me that Roosevelt was still much loved in Britain, and that his country had stood alone against the German onslaught for nearly two years before America entered the war. Perhaps, he said, I should visit Coventry Cathedral to see what the English had suffered.

Sometime later my wife Sue and I invited the Ramseys to our apartment for dinner. The Ramseys had been frequent visitors to many of the students' homes, and we looked forward anxiously to their visit. We knew of their fondness for stews, something we could manage, and of the Bishop's enjoyment of cream sherry and beer. That evening was a Thursday, the day when Nashotah House always celebrated a community Eucharist replete with "smells and bells," and we had a guest preacher, a well-known charismatic priest from Houston. During the sermon the priest made some fulsome remarks about the one-hundredth Archbishop of Canterbury in our midst, who was the greatest of them all since Thomas à Becket. At this point and for the remainder of a long rambling, insufferable sermon, Ramsey was seen shaking his head, rolling his eyes, holding his head in his hands, and groaning and sighing audibly.

Just as soon as he and Lady Ramsey settled in the car for the drive to our apartment, he exploded with anger: "These charismatics go on and on like that! They don't know much of anything, but assume the Holy Spirit is telling them what to say. That fellow had no point to make, except to talk, blah, blah, blah! He thinks if he mentions Jesus' name a few hundred times he's preached the Gospel. Always worried about their warm feelings, always about feelings. Butler said it well, 'This pretending to the Holy Spirit is a very horrid thing, a very horrid thing.' And what does he know about Archbishops of Canterbury? Has he ever heard of Langton? Or of Parker? Or of either Temple? Randall Davidson? The Holy Spirit probably told him to say those things tonight!"

At that point I wondered how the evening would turn out, but the Ramseys put us completely at ease. It would be hard to find more amiable guests. Neither one was the least concerned about being fashionable;

the Bishop frequently wore his purple cassock with black buckled shoes, and he had a green down jacket for colder weather, while on formal occasions he dressed in a black suit. (This was a purple cassock evening.) They lived a frugal, almost spartan existence. Our student apartment with "early Salvation Army" furniture was fine as far as they were concerned. The only disconcerting moment was when Ramsey suddenly broke into a hymn, which occurred when the subject of our conversation had switched to one of interest to the rest of us, but not one of theology, politics, history, or a social or moral matter that engaged his attention. He did refer once to his earlier outburst about the charismatic preacher, perhaps by way of making amends, remarking that the only churches that seemed to be growing in the Church of England were evangelical and charismatic.

A few years later, Bishop Ramsey preached at my ordination to the priesthood at Grace Church, Madison, Wisconsin, the only time, he said, when he had done so in the Episcopal Church. My wife and I saw the Ramseys again in 1982 when we visited England and made the pilgrimage, as so many of his former students did, to see the Ramseys in Durham. Just before we left them, he asked us if we had seen the cloister at Canterbury Cathedral where William Temple was buried. He hoped, he said, to be buried next to him. He worried, though, that because of his decision to be cremated, future visitors might mistake the small canister labelled "Michael" to be Temple's pet cat.

Shortly after arriving back from our first trip to Britain, I wrote Ramsey inquiring as to any plans he might have in publishing some lectures he had given at Nashotah House during my senior year in the fall of 1979. I strongly believed they would prove beneficial to the church both as an introduction to Anglicanism and to Ramsey's own theology. I had enjoyed them immensely, and in conversations with many fellow students I heard them speaking of Hooker and Newman for the first time, with intentions to follow up with further reading on the ideas and personalities treated by Ramsey. Why not publish the lectures and add notes from Ramsey's works and other books for those who wished to pursue various subjects?

Ramsey tentatively agreed, and asked to see transcriptions I had made from the tapes of the lectures he had given from notes. It took some time to carry this out, but I sent him the material as I transcribed it. He thought they might be worthy of publication, but he was very leery of doing so since a recent book of his, *Jesus and the Living Past*, also taken from lectures, had been poorly received. He liked the material, but saw that much work would be necessary in editing it for book form. I arranged to visit him in August of 1986 to assist him in any way possible.

With my mother I traveled to Durham in late August to find the Ramseys in some distress as they were in the final process of packing for their move to Bishopthorpe, the Archbishop of York's residence, where they would live in a cottage on the grounds. A few days before they had been in an automobile accident; their taxicab was struck from behind in a roundabout near their Durham home. While we were received with great kindness and enjoyed lively discussions at lunch and dinner about the Falklands War, the political abilities of Prime Minister Margaret Thatcher, and Archbishop Runcie's response to both, Bishop Ramsey seemed at times depressed over his weakening physical state since the accident. He could only read with great effort, using a large magnifying glass, and he experienced frequent headaches. He did not believe he would ever have the energy to do all the work of editing he wished in order to put the lectures in publishable form. I suggested to him that part of the charm of the lectures was their conversational flavor. Paul Tillich's lectures on the history of Christian thought had been transcribed and published posthumously in 1966, with the inclusion of Tillich's humorous remarks and responses to students' questions. Could this be a possibility also for the lectures? "Perhaps, perhaps", was Ramsey's reply, with the excising of most of the "little jokes" that were of local interest only. That was the last time I spoke with Michael Ramsey.

The Anglican Spirit

MY PURPOSE IN this book is to discuss the historical origin of Anglicanism, not doing over again what has been covered so well by so many others, but rather reminding ourselves of that historical setting in which it all began. Then I want to talk about some of the main enduring characteristics of Anglican tradition, the way in which the Anglican Church has in its life and teaching, theology and sacraments, given over that divine "paradosis"—which is the Greek word for something that has been "handed over" or "passed on." For when we Christians speak of tradition, we mean the experience of the Christian community lying authentically within that which God through Christ has handed over for the revelation of himself and the salvation of men and women everywhere. Then I shall talk about certain select doctrines and certain select great Anglican personalities, and finish by mentioning my own hopes for the future of the Anglican way of life and faith.

But first let us have a reminder of our historical setting. King Henry VIII had six wives. Not every English schoolchild could recite the names of the six correctly, but nearly every English schoolchild will know the rhyme about their fate: "Divorced, beheaded, died./ Divorced, beheaded, survived." One might wonder already what on earth that has got to do with our present church! The answer is, it has got everything to do with who we are. Because again and again, it is through apparently chance events that divine providence works in order to bring about great religious situations and subsequent great religious manifestations. And so it is in this case. Indeed, those six wives are well worth commemorating.

What in fact happened? King Henry VIII was dissatisfied with the first of those wives because she was not successful in producing a male heir for him. There had been some possible irregularity about the marriage, so that fair-minded people thought the marriage could be annulled. Henry assumed the Pope would annull his marriage, but in order to accomplish his purpose, he had eventually to break with the papacy and substitute himself as the head—or supreme governor—of the English church. Simply put, that was the beginning of the Church of England as a national phenomemon dissociated from the papacy; it was the beginning of the royal supremacy which for some time, in practice and in theory, has remained part of the Anglican Church in the country from which I come.

Now we have to warn ourselves at this point against what used to be an Anglo-Catholic oversimplification. People who should know better say that this meant no change in religion, for religion went on just as it was—the Catholic faith minus the Pope. In a sense that was true because King Henry, apart from abolishing the monasteries (which had become very corrupt institutions) was staunchly conservative in relation to Catholic faith. Please recall that the Pope had even given him the title of "Defender of the Faith."[1] But it was not as simple as all that, for this reason: the difference between a Christianity that can make do without the papacy is already a Christianity in which changes of belief and sentiment are taking place.

So I think it is true to say that in Henry's reign, while there was officially no radical change in doctrine or in the sentiments of the people or in the feeling of the country, the Lutheran reformation was already having its impact. We can see this in two ways. First, the English Bible was not issued to merely a few fanatics, but rather commended officially to be read to the people and made available in the churches. That development is inconceivable apart from a strong Lutheran influence in the country.

In the second place, there was a considerable change in the concept of the royal supremacy itself. Royal supremacy was indeed a doctrine, a powerful Reformation doctrine derived from Martin Luther. It did not mean that the monarch was a source of revelation, nor that the monarch was a doctrinal authority. It did mean, however, that it was for the monarch to say what sort of church, and what style of authority and doctrine, was desirable for the people to accept.

Now we must press on rapidly because we are only reminding ourselves of certain facts and background details. Henry VIII was followed by King Edward VI, in whose reign further steps toward reformation took place with the guidance of Archbishop Cranmer. The first Prayer Book of Archbishop Cranmer in 1549 produced a liturgy quite remarkably like the one we pray even today. And in that reformed liturgy, while he was deliberately steering away from what was understood at the time to be Catholic notions of sacrifice, Cranmer deliberately conserved the doctrine of the presence and gift of the Lord himself in the sacrament through the words, "The body of our Lord Jesus Christ which was given for thee, preserve thy body and soul unto everlasting life." The 1549 Prayer Book spoke of ministering the cup to the people. Moreover, in Cranmer's hands, the liturgy became something in which the people participate—as distinct from a ritual that the priest carried on while the people watched.

But the trend of Reformation doctrine and study on the Continent had moved on considerably, and so there were now a large number of Calvinists and Zwinglian scholars in the country holding posts in the English universities. Therefore it came about that three years later Cranmer's second Prayer Book, the 1552 Prayer Book, was considerably more Protestant—in fact, Calvinistic-Zwinglian—in tone. The eucharistic canon was broken up into two parts, while the words, "The body of our Lord Jesus Christ...preserve thy body and soul unto everlasting life", were dropped and replaced by the memorialist formula, "Take and eat this, in remembrance that Christ died for thee," which was indeed the doctrine that caused Martin Luther to bang the table in protest when he was arguing with Zwingli about those matters.[2]

A strong reaction came about under Queen Mary, who married King Philip of Spain. There was a return to full-bodied Roman Catholicism and the ghastly martyrdom by burning of Archbishop Cranmer and a number of those who had left the Roman Catholic Church under King Henry and King Edward. I think it is fair to say that the Marian Roman Catholic interlude, while it checked for a time the advance of continental Protestant divinity in the English schools, had the effect of evoking feelings of intense nationalism in England, along with no less passionate feelings of anti-popery.

I really want to start in 1558 with Queen Elizabeth and the Elizabethan Settlement, and I have sketched in the background very rapidly in this early history just to indicate that there was something for Queen Elizabeth to settle. You only settle things if there is something to settle, namely, what sort of Christianity was the country going to have? What sort of church was the country going to have? It was for Queen Elizabeth herself to initiate policy because both she and her parliament believed strongly in the royal supremacy. What sort of church was it to be? Not a church invented by her, because royal supremacy did not mean that. Not a church with doctrines invented by her, or revealed through her, because royal supremacy did not mean that.

No, it was the Christian church as it had always been despite these changes, still possessing the Holy Scriptures, the creeds, the sacraments of baptism, confirmation, the Eucharist, and the three-fold ministry of bishops, priests and deacons. Because Queen Elizabeth took good care that those appointed bishops were consecrated by those who were bishops already, maintaining a succession that had run right through all the troubles I have been describing—it was the same Christian church. The language of its worship was still about the One, Holy Catholic Church in this land, represented by a body of bishops and clergy at their head, possessing a real continuity that had prevailed through all these ups and downs.

But it was necessary for someone to give theological interpretation and shape and content to this fact of the Settlement, to this fact of the Elizabethan church. At this point, in 1559, there comes on to the scene the figure of Matthew Parker, the first Archbishop of Canterbury in the Elizabethan reign.

Matthew Parker was youngish, an academic who had been master of Corpus Christi College, Cambridge. He was a man devoted to great learning. Before I mention some of the practical things he did, let me tell you about the way he used his learning, because he used it in a way that might have seemed highly irrelevant in those times, but in fact proved to be gloriously relevant. Parker collected Anglo-Saxon manuscripts about the life of the country and the life of the church in the centuries between Augustine of Canterbury and the Norman conquest. He amassed this collection, classified and edited it, and had it copied. Finally, just before he died, Parker saw to it that the collection was kept not in his home at Lambeth, but handed over to his college, Corpus Christi at Cambridge, a very fortunate thing, because the former was bombed in the last war and the latter was not. (Here is one of these little pieces of perhaps providential guidance.)

Why this interest in Anglo-Saxon manuscripts? Parker wanted to show that a number of features of the Elizabethan church were not new inventions, but familiar to the Catholic church in England in its earlier centuries. Public worship in the vernacular, allowing clergymen to marry, detachment from obedience to the Pope, believing that the Lord was present in the Holy Communion while steering away from the development toward transubstantiation of the early Middle Ages—all these developments were revealed by Parker's manuscripts. In fact, this collection was designed to show that the Church of England was not *de novo*. Some of its forms and some of its relationships to other bodies had to be newly described and defined, but at the heart of the matter—its gospel, its creeds, its sacraments, its ministry, and a good deal of its customs—it was essentially the same church. And that is what is sometimes called the Anglican appeal to antiquity.

Now Parker did even more than that. Documents and formularies were needed to define the church in its contemporary state. Through the Act of Uniformity, royal supremacy already required the restored Prayer Book to be in use. While this restored Prayer Book dated from 1552 rather than 1549, it restored Cranmer's original words of administration: "The body of our Lord Jesus Christ...preserve thy body and soul unto everlasting life." Queen Elizabeth herself was something of a theologian, and to her are attributed some verses about the Eucharist that certainly express the intention of the church of her time:

> Christ was the word who spake it,
> Christ took the bread and brake it,
> And what his word doth make it,
> That I believe and take it.

Trusting that because Christ says so, Christ truly is present, and Christ gives his own self to us as his gift. That was Queen Elizabeth, and that was the Prayer Book she used.

When it came to orders, it was undoubtedly the wish of the Queen and of Archbishop Parker that the church adhere to the basic Christian tradition, the primitive Christian *paradosis* interpreted as widely as possible to include everyone except definite Romanists, Calvinists, and Anabaptists. The Calvinists, of course, were now not only divines on the Continent, but also Puritans growing up on English soil.

Now for those documents that would define the contemporary church—the 1571 *Thirty-Nine Articles*, *The Second Book of Homilies*, and the "Canon of Preaching." Here I will trespass on the ground of your instructors in systematic theology, who will have pointed out to you that the *Thirty-Nine Articles* indeed owe something to Luther in their strong emphasis on justification by faith, but reject what came to be called "solifidianism"—the belief that works have no value in the Christian life. It is also equally clear that much importance is attached to election or predestination, but the *Articles* definitely avoid Calvin's unattractive doctrine of double predestination to salvation or damnation.

It is important to notice that while other churches on the Continent with Reformation roots also had their sets of articles, the Anglican Settlement as now defined had not only a confession, a set of articles, but also a Prayer Book. It is this foundation that was, and remains, so very characteristic of the Anglican *paradosis*. And it is true to say that while there are churches in Christendom where, when you ask, "Now, tell us what you stand for?" they will say, "Well here are our articles, that is what we stand for," it has always been characteristic of Anglicans to reply, "Yes, here are our articles, but here is our Prayer Book as well—come and pray with us, come and worship with us, and that is how you will understand what we stand for." That is something that we are going to find recurring again and again in all the ups and downs of the Anglican *paradosis*.

Up to this point, there could not be a distinctive and articulate Anglican theology. When people are wrestling hard with the kinds of practical questions the Elizabethan Settlement raised, they have not the leisure for a great deal of profound reflection. So I think it is more true to say that the Elizabethan Settlement was not the product of theology, but of a desire to cling to the primitive church and to define certain limits. That being so, there still remained something to theologize about. Anglican theology followed the Elizabethan Settlement, rather than the other way around. Distinctive Anglican theology began within the reign of the first Queen Elizabeth, and has continued ever since. To see it emerging, I think we have to look not only at Hooker and the Elizabethan divines, but also at the Caroline divines of the next century, and to go on looking at every subsequent century after that.

Richard Hooker lived in the latter part of Elizabeth's reign, and he spent most of his ministry as a parish priest. He held for some years the post of Master of the Temple—the church in London where lawyers, judges, and so on worship—but his greater role was as a parish priest, and he died the rector of the parish of Bishopsbourne near Canterbury.

Characteristically, Hooker's work was not a treatise on theology simply for its own sake, but rather a polemical discussion of the controversies between the Anglican Church and the Puritans. Its title, *Laws of Ecclesiastical Polity*,[3] shows that. But in this writing of Hooker we find emerging certain powerful Anglican characteristics. So rather than describe Hooker's teaching as a whole, I am just going to pick from it certain things already characteristic of the Anglican mode of *paradosis* that continues through the centuries.

First of all, the close connection between theology, doctrine, and Christian worship is very powerful in Hooker. He describes what we believe very much in terms of how we worship. That has remained a characteristic of Anglican theology right into the present century, and German theologians, very rigorous in their academic method, have sometimes laughed at Anglican theologians for doing their theology to the sound of church bells. Well, continue to do theology to the sound of church bells, for that is what Christian theology really is all about—worshipping God the Savior through Jesus Christ in the theology of the apostolic age.

A second characteristic of Hooker is a belief in authority mingled with a great distrust of infallibility. He is ready to believe, certainly, in what God has shown and done, but equally ready to shrink from claims for the infallibility of the language in which God's revelation is at any time expressed. A sentence of Hooker expresses this: "Two things there are that trouble these latter times: one is that the Church of Rome cannot, another is that Geneva will not, err." This remains an honest Anglican characteristic, and if we want to unravel it, I think we need to probe into religious language and the extent to which its use is inevitable in expressing divine relationship, although not in making a mathematical statement.

A sense of mystery and of the mysteriousness of divine truth is something Hooker felt very strongly indeed. Again and again we find him pausing and saying, "Do not ask me to define it, do not define it yourself, it really is truly mysterious." And he combined that sense of mystery with a real certainty about what God has given through Christ and in the church. Here again, unravelling the implications of Hooker's sense of mystery still leaves a lot of probing to be done.

Let me recall to you Hooker's famous passage about the eucharistic presence, where he expresses how mysterious it is that Christ really does give to us his own body and blood, he really does give to us a gift that unites us to him in his passion. Yet how wrong it is to ask too many questions when we are faced with the joy of his wonderful and mysterious gift. This is a fine instance both of the style of Hooker's language and of this mode of mystery in his thinking. It is a very moving passage:

> Let it therefore be sufficient for me presenting myself at the Lord's table to know what there I receive from him, without searching or inquiring of the manner of how Christ performeth His promise....Let curious and sharp-witted men beat their heads about what questions themselves will, the very letter of the word of Christ giveth plain security that these mysteries do as nails fasten us to his very cross, that by them we draw out, as touching efficacy, force, and virtue, even the blood of his pierced side, in the wounds of our Redeemer we there dip our tongues, we are dyed red both within and without, our hunger is satisfied, and our thirst forever quenched; they are things wonderful which

he feeleth, great which he seeth, and unheard of
which he uttereth, whose soul is possessed of this
paschal lamb, and made joyful in the strength of
this new wine....What these elements are in themselves it skilleth not, it is enough that to me which
take them they are the body and blood of Christ, his
promise in witness hereof sufficeth, his word he
knoweth which way to accomplish; why should any
cogitation possess the mind of a faithful communicant but this, *O my God thou art true, O my soul
thou art happy?*[4]

The final characteristic of Hooker's thought I would
like to mention is this: divine revelation does not
address itself to human souls in a kind of vacuum or
by a take-it-or-leave it process. No, the natural order
is God's own creation. There is a divine reason present
in the universe, operating in lots of different ways,
whereby God bears witness to His own presence and
activity. This indwelling of divine reason in the
created world operates especially in the mind and the
conscience of men and women. Thus revelation is a
divine activity that evokes and calls for our own
powers of reason and conscience, because those
powers of reason and conscience are themselves God-
given.

That aspect of revelation is strongly present in
Hooker's *Laws*, which no doubt you will be studying,
and recurs in Anglican divines whose strong belief in
God known through revelation does not deny the role
of God in nature. For what God does in revelation
brings to a climax what God does in nature; what God
does in nature is a necessary key to the understanding of what God does in revelation. It was that
line of thought, I think, that tended to push the Incarnation into first place in Anglican theology. It would
be a bit of an oversimplification to say (but perhaps
not too much of one) that in Anglican theology

through the centuries the Incarnation has been a more central and prominent doctrine than that of the cross and redemption, and certainly more so than justification or predestination.

These aspects of Hooker's thinking came to characterize Anglican tradition throughout the centuries— but not because Anglican divines had all come out of Hooker factories, or had been disciples of Hooker in the same way that Lutherans are disciples of Luther and Calvinists of Calvin. Rather, I honestly believe that the Elizabethan Settlement by the nature of its appeal to Scripture and antiquity, and by its relationship to the contemporary controversies, liberated theology to appeal to Scripture and tradition in a way that could be really creative, and it is going to be our great task to see that it remains so.

Scripture, Antiquity, and Reason

I N THE PREVIOUS chapter we discussed the Anglican tradition, and how this tradition, which was delivered to the world by God through Christ, is passed on through the Anglican Church in its teaching, its life, and its theology. We also saw that after the Elizabethan Settlement, certain characteristics of Anglican theology began to emerge. I would now like to pursue that theme by examining the Anglican appeal to Scripture, antiquity, and reason.

First, then, the appeal to Holy Scripture. The Anglican Church has always regarded and still regards Holy Scripture as the supreme authority for the doctrine of the Christian Church. Article Six of the *Thirty-Nine Articles* is called "Of the Sufficiency of the Holy Scriptures for Salvation," and has this to say: "Scripture containeth all things necessary to salvation, so that whatsoever is not read therein nor may be proved thereby is not required of any man that it should be believed as an article of faith or thought to be necessary for salvation." Article Seven continues, "The Old Testament is not contrary to the New, for both in the Old and in the New everlasting life is offered to mankind by Christ, who is the only mediator between God and Man, being both God and man."

The supremacy of Holy Scripture, therefore, is related to the salvation of the human race. This emphasis on the sufficiency of Scripture is itself a "hit" at the Roman Catholic Council of Trent, which used language suggesting that a body of truth existed in antiquity outside of Holy Scripture, and that this body of truth has been handed down to the church. In other words, the Council claimed that there was a source of authority directly from Christ and the Apostles in addition to the authority of Holy Scripture, and it was against that idea that the *Thirty-Nine Articles* protested.

But we must notice most of all their emphasis upon the need for salvation. Holy Scripture contains truth necessary for *salvation*. The Articles do not say that Holy Scripture contains truth on innumerable subjects not related to salvation, and here we have the difference between the treatment of Scripture by the Anglicans, as represented by Hooker, and by the Puritans. The Anglicans claimed that whatever is needed for our salvation we find in Scripture, but we do not necessarily have to follow Scripture for rules concerning the details of the life of the church. The Puritans, *per contra*, insisted that Holy Scripture does provide necessary rules and details for the life of the Church.

Two examples, one actual and the other hypothetical. The Anglicans used a ring in the sacrament of Holy Marriage because there is nothing that forbids it and it seems a devout and good custom. The Puritans said no, a ring in marriage is not ordered by Holy Scripture and therefore it is wrong to use it. To cite another, more hypothetical instance: when Anglicans use incense in public worship, they do so because it appears to be a holy and edifying custom with evident symbolism attached to it. But Anglicans would not say that the use of incense in public worship is biblically ordered simply because its use is described in the Book of Revelation. Scripture tells us what is necessary for salvation, but it is not a source of authority for countless other things as well. Hooker has a striking passage about this. In his *Laws of Ecclesiastical*

Polity, he notes that Holy Scripture must not be used for the kinds of information and knowledge of information that it is not concerned about, because that knowledge and information does not bear upon salvation.[1]

In the second of the Articles quoted above, it stated that the Old Testament is not contrary to the New because in both salvation is offered to humanity through Jesus Christ. How is salvation offered through the Old Testament as well as through the New Testament? Again, Hooker has something to say about this. In a passage that comes a little later than the one I quoted above, he speaks of how the Old Testament reveals Christ by pointing the way to him as the fulfiller, while the New Testament reveals Christ as the one who fulfills what is shadowed in the Old.

How do we understand that doctrine today? There are in the Old Testament a number of passages that may seem strange to us or even cause considerable mirth. For example, portions of Leviticus, or stories in the Elijah and Elisha cycles found in 1 and 2 Kings may strike many of us as odd. How can passages of such mirth and apparent irrelevance bear upon the salvation of humankind through Jesus Christ?

I believe that the concept is both intelligible and true. How does God save the world? God saves the world by manifesting Himself through the divine *Logos*, through seers and thinkers and the consciences of men and women far and wide. More specifically, God saves the world by manifesting Himself to Israel. And the life of Israel and the revelation to Israel is a great divine work preparing the way for Christ. In that work of God revealing Himself to Israel, the whole life of the people is involved—the follies and backslidings and absurdities as well as the virtues and great deeds of righteousness. In the whole drama of the Bible, with all its ups and downs, God is

manifesting Himself as the righteous savior God in a
way that points to Christ, and is incomplete without
Christ. Thus everything that lies within both the Old
and New Testaments is a part of that drama of salvation of which Christ is the head and the climax. In
that sense it is true indeed that the Scriptures are a
unity to which Christ is the key.

But how is Scripture to be interpreted? Who will be
the guide to our understanding? For is it likely that
Holy Scripture will be rightly understood in a kind of
vacuum? This leads us to the second part of the Anglican appeal, the Anglican appeal to antiquity, the appeal to ancient tradition.

Article Twenty of the *Articles of Religion* describes
the church as the witness to and keeper of Holy Writ.
In that belief, the Anglican divines looked increasingly to the Fathers of the ancient church as guides to
the understanding of Scripture. Here is a classic passage about how the appeal to Scripture and the appeal
to ancient tradition go together in Anglican thinking.
The writer is one Francis White and the work is called
A Treatise of the Sabbath Day, written in 1635.

> The Church of England in her public and
> authorized Doctrine and Religion proceedeth in
> manner following. It buildeth her faith and religion
> upon the Sacred Canonical Scriptures...[But] next
> to the Holy Scripture, it relieth upon the consen-
> tient testimony and authority of the bishops and pa-
> stors of the true and ancient Catholic Church; and
> it preferreth the sentence therof before all other
> curious and profane novelties. [Thus] the Holy
> Scripture is the fountain and lively spring, contain-
> ing in all sufficiency the pure water of life...The
> consentient and unanimous testimony of the true
> church of Christ in the primitive ages...is *canalis*, a
> conduit pipe, to derive and convey to succeeding
> generations the celestial water contained in Holy

Scripture. The first of these, namely Scripture, is the sovereign authority...The latter is a ministerial and subordinant rule and guide to preserve and direct us to the right understanding of the Scriptures.[2]

A similar appeal to the tradition of antiquity was made forcibly in the "Canon on Preaching," a canon issued in 1571 at the same time as the *Thirty-Nine Articles*. And this "Canon on Preaching" states that the preachers in the churches should preach nothing but what is found in Holy Scripture and what the ancient fathers and catholic doctors have collected from the same. That is to say, antiquity is regarded as a guide to the understanding of Scripture. The classic ancient definition of this authority of the church of antiquity is found in St. Vincent, who said that the church's understanding be directed by "what has been believed everywhere, always, by all—*quod ubique, quod semper, quod ab omnibus creditum est.*" Therefore the interpretation of Holy Scripture is to be found in what Christians, the members of the church, believe always, everywhere, and by all.

Now, this appeal to the ancient Fathers became increasingly characteristic of Anglican thought. It became as well the point of divergence between characteristic Anglican theology and the theology of the Lutheran and Calvinistic churches on the Continent. This trend, which was of immense interest in the teaching of the Fathers, came to be called by the broad umbrella word of "Arminian." Jacobus Arminius was a Dutch Protestant who quarreled with the official Calvinist teaching on a number of points, such as the predestination of some to damnation, and the irresistible character of God's grace. In quarreling with the official Calvinist line, he came to be regarded by the Calvinists as a heretic. But his teaching, a greatly modified Calvinism, spread widely, and spread considerably into the Anglican Church. It remained very powerful in the Anglican Church for some time, as we can see from a rather whimsical conversation reported to have taken place in the seventeenth century. Question: "Can you tell me what the Arminians hold?" Answer: "I am sorry to say that they hold half the deaneries in England!"

Thus the word "Arminian" came to be a rather vague description of the Anglican divines who were not Calvinist, but High Church, sacramental, devoted to antiquity, and perhaps Pelagian. It is also a word that has stuck in Anglican history for a very long time, lasting right down to the Methodist movement, when it was aptly noted that of the two great leaders of the Methodist revival, one of them, George Whitefield, was Calvinist and the other, John Wesley, was an Arminian. Wesley would not have rejected the description because it broadly represented his position.

What, then, was the effect upon Anglican theology of this increasing devotion to antiquity, to the church fathers, and to the authority of antiquity as a guide to the right interpretation of Holy Scripture? The effect certainly was, and perhaps still is, to give a certain archaic flavor to Anglican theology. Besides that, there were effects of a very creative kind. Christian antiquity is both Latin and Greek, both western and eastern, and the Anglican appeal to antiquity meant that Greek as well as Latin theology came to figure largely in the Anglican consciousness and in the work of Anglican divines. I remind you of the prayer included in Lancelot Andrewes' book of prayers: "Let us pray for the whole church; eastern, western, our own...."[3] To live with that point of view—the church is eastern, western, and our own—had, of course, a broadening as well as archaizing effect upon the ethos of Anglican divinity. Furthermore, the Anglican devotion to antiquity helped it get right away from medieval and post-medieval controversies and see some of those controverted questions in a larger perspective.

Let me give two examples, the first being the doctrine of the Eucharist. In the sixteenth century, understandings of the Eucharist came to be terribly bogged down between a very lop-sided medieval conception of the meaning of sacrifice in the Mass, over against a tendency to reject the concept of sacrifice in the Mass totally in reaction to the corrupt medieval idea. Of course it was possible for both sides to quote Scripture, although merely quoting Scripture did not provide the answer. Yet Anglican divinity, because of its devotion to the ancient fathers, found it possible to see this controversy in a larger perspective and explore a concept of sacrifice that neither fully embraced it nor rejected it, as many of the reformers did. That is an instance of how the Anglican appeal to antiquity could be a creative source of synthesis, a new valuation and progress.

Another illustration comes from the doctrine of the Communion of Saints, which holds that the souls in paradise and the saints in heaven are one family of prayer and worship with the church here on earth. They are one family reflecting the unique glory of Jesus. Now at the time of the Reformation controversies, there was on the one hand a medieval doctrine of purgatory of a very corrupt kind, and on the other a doctrine of devotion to the saints that made the saints, as it were, individual mediators who supplemented the mediatorship of Jesus. In reaction, people began to insist that all prayers for the departed must be wrong, while all sense of praying and worshipping with the saints in heaven was wrong as well, because it interfered with the unique prerogative of Jesus.

Because of its devotion to antiquity, Anglican divinity has been able to get away from that false antithesis and recover thought and teaching about the

Communion of Saints. It has been able to recover the kind of teaching that is found, for instance, in St. John Chrysostom, where you have the church on earth, the souls in paradise, the saints in heaven, and the Blessed Virgin Mary as a family unity of mutual prayer and thanksgiving. The Communion of Saints is the reflection of the unique glory of Jesus in those who belong to him on earth, or in paradise, or in heaven.

These are two instances in which the Anglican appeal to antiquity, for all its archaisms and frequent pedantry and apparent retrogression, has been something that makes for peace and synthesis and creativity. It was the glory of the Anglican appeal to antiquity that it included the ancient East as well the ancient West, and that continues today.

Now, alongside its appeal to Scripture and antiquity, Anglicanism also makes an appeal to reason. This third kind of appeal is a little difficult to define, and its manifestations have been buried in different phases of Anglican history. God created the human race, not in a vacuum, but as part of a created order in which He manifests Himself. And in the created order, the divine *logos* is a principle of unity and purpose and rationality. Through the indwelling of the divine *logos* in the world, it informs the conscience and the reason of men and women. Quite outside the biblical covenants, therefore, we have the rudiments of a knowledge of God through that conscience and reason that are bestowed by Him.

This principle of the indwelling *logos* includes our perception of right and wrong. By virtue of that perception we are able to know shape and purpose, as well as model order, in the universe. That knowledge is hazardous and incomplete until revelation comes to crown it, indeed, until redemption comes to cleanse us, so that our conscience and reason may be freed from those things that thwart and corrupt them.

Now this appeal to reason, which takes place in the context of the biblical revelation and the appeal to antiquity, has appeared in Anglican history in a number of forms. Let me mention two or three instances of the powerful Anglican appeal to reason that you may care to follow up on your own.

One example comes from those divines in the seventeenth century called the Cambridge Platonists,[4] a group that flourished roughly between 1630 and 1690. The Cambridge Platonists were very aware of the role of reason in religion, and of the presence of the divine Spirit in nature and in human beings. A single, much-quoted sentence of one of their number, Benjamin Whichcote, really expresses and defines the character of their work. He wrote, "The spirit in man is the candle of the Lord."[5] That sentence draws together both the quest for the divine through the use of human reason studying the world, and the quest for the divine through a mystical experience of God in the indwelling Spirit. Among them, the study of Plato's writings to supplement Holy Scripture was typical of the way these scholars worked.

In the eighteenth century, a good instance of the Anglican appeal to reason is found in the work of Joseph Butler replying to the Deists of his time. I strongly recommend the study not only of Butler's sermons, but also of his great work, *The Analogy of Religion*.[6] Butler applied the concept of reason to human worship, in contrast with the more rationalistic view of his time that ignored the presence of the Spirit of God in human reason.

For us today, however, perhaps the most significant aspect of the Anglican appeal to reason is found in the nineteenth century crisis of faith, a crisis both for Anglicans and for all Christians. At that time, the development of the scientific revolution appeared to be challenging the authority of Holy Scripture. In reaction to this challenge, church people began to treat Holy Scripture in ways that the Anglican formularies did not require and that Richard Hooker certainly would have repudiated. The Bible was used not merely to declare the things necessary to salvation, but also as a source of information on every conceivable subject: geology, botany, astronomy, biology, the rotation of the world, and the details of human history through the centuries.

A literalist view of the Bible, which was common to Anglicans and to Christians of almost every sort, came to be challenged by the growth of sciences, geology, and biology. Literal-minded churchmen claimed that the world had been created in exactly six days, with the creation of the two first parents as its climax. The discoveries of biology, geology, and other sciences, however, held that the human race was the result of a long evolutionary process. Hence a clash between a literalistic view of the Bible and a developing science.

Another clash occurred between what was held to be the historical character of all the biblical records, and the application of historical criticism to ancient documents. So it became very hard to believe that everything described in the Pentateuch, for instance, is literal history, and for many this brought about a crisis of faith. Yet the appeal to reason as a God-given attribute made it possible for believers to realize that the divine *logos* is at work in the sciences themselves—in the new understanding of nature that produced the evolutionary theories, in the new historical study that challenged the literal character of every biblical narrative.

That being so, Christian theology can continue its belief in divine creation and in biblical revelation—

not in diminished, but in wonderfully enhanced ways. Thus the work of the divine creator is no less glorious if God in fact created the world through a slow evolving process with human beings as the climax. Equally, the Bible is not diminished but enhanced if God's revelation is not limited to prosaic literal statements, but able to use poetry, drama, symbol, imagery, and a whole wealth of literary forms of speech and thought in showing His existence, His graciousness, and His purposes to humanity. The drama of the Book of Job, and perhaps the poetry of the Book of Jonah, can be no less revealing of God's glory and beauty than are literal statements.

Now those are some significant instances of how the Anglican tradition appealed to Scripture as containing all things necessary to salvation, to antiquity as a guide to the understanding of Scripture, and to reason as a God-given faculty for receiving divine revelation. Reason increases and enlarges human understanding of divine revelation through its own workings, so long as reason is used in humble dependence upon the God who gave it.

The Anglican tradition has continued to be a kind of triangle, a kind of balance between the appeals to Scripture, tradition, reason. And it is possible for the three sides of that triangle to pull apart. Inevitably there have been within the Anglican churches those who have specially emphasized the appeal to Scripture, and have not bothered very much about the ancient Fathers. There have been those who have appealed strongly to ancient tradition, but might have paid a little more attention to Holy Scripture, and perhaps a little more attention to reason as well. There have also been those who, concentrating upon the activity of God in reason, have not been quite as sensitive as they might be to what is revealed in Holy Scripture and contemptuous of traditions as something that old men used to think many, many centuries ago.

This division of emphasis is entirely healthy if kept a matter merely of emphasis, but it can become partisan and divisive if pursued recklessly. So we occasionally witness not just the appeal to scripture, but a kind of scripturalism, and any "ism" can be dangerous. Scripturalism is not the same thing as the appeal to Holy Scripture. Traditionalism is not the same thing as the intelligent appeal to tradition. And rationalism can be a very evil thing when it involves a worship of reason, and forgets that reason is concerned with great mysteries requiring awe, wonder, and even cleverness. Reason itself is a gift of God; its use can be corrupted if our dependence upon God is forgotten. So we in our study of the Anglican tradition must pursue the ways that the appeal to Scripture, tradition, and reason can still mutually enrich one another.

Cultural and Political Anglicanism

WE HAVE CONSIDERED the emergence of the Anglican tradition, its theological character in terms of its appeal to Scripture, antiquity, and reason, and for the rest of these lectures we will be looking at some of the theological and spiritual resources of the Anglican tradition in its great teachers of the past. No religious tradition exists in a vacuum; all religious traditions have a political and cultural context. So this lecture is about cultural and political Anglicanism, because we must be aware both of the influence of that setting upon it and of its influence upon that setting.

In boasting of being a *via media*, a "middle way" between two extremes, and in having the intellectual and literary standards of the Cranmerian Prayer Book, Anglicanism was inevitably vulnerable to criticism. Many saw it as a religion for the educated class, a faith for the sophisticated rather than for the masses.

A particularly striking and sardonic expression of this criticism was made by Mark Pattison, a nineteenth-century theologian. Mark Pattison was originally a Tractarian and a disciple of John Henry Newman, but he swung violently away from that allegiance and became something of a rasping critic not only of that particular tradition, but of the Anglican Church in general. Pattison wrote these words:

> Anglicanism has always been the religion of the educated classes exclusively. It has never at any period been national and popular, because it implies more historical information and a wider horizon than can be possessed by the peasant and artisan. The masses require an intuitional religion such as is provided by the grosser forms of dissent in Great Britain, or a ceremonial drill and parade such as the Latin and Greek Churches offer to their subject populations.[1]

If those words are something of a caricature, they are not wholly unfair; if you boast of the *via media* as your ideal, you can not grumble if you are critized for mediocrity. Indeed, in its earlier phases, Anglicanism used to boast of this cultural quality. In a famous poem, the seventeenth-century poet George Herbert describes three ladies, one very overdressed lady (and you know who she would be), one naked lady (and you know who she would be), and a lady just properly clad, which is the Anglican *via media*:

> A fine aspect in fit array,
> Neither too mean, nor yet too gay,
>   Shows who is best.
> Outlandish looks may not compare:
> For all they either painted are,
>   Or else undrest.
>
> She on the hills, which wantonly
> Allureth all in hope to be
>   By her preferr'd
> Hath kiss'd so long her painted shrines,
> That ev'n her face by kissing shines,
>   For her reward.
>
> She in the valley is so shie
> Of dressing, that her hair doth lie

About her eares:
While she avoids her neighbours pride,
She wholly goes on th' other side,
    And nothing wears.

But, dearest Mother, what those misse,
The mean, thy praise and glorie is,
    And long may be.
Blessed be God, whose love it was
To double-moat thee with his grace,
    And none but thee.[2]

That is the evidence of a feeling of ethical and cultural superiority that keeps on recurring in Anglican history. I forget who it was who summed it up in a single prose sentence: the Anglican Church steers a middle course between the squalid slattery of fanatic conventicles and the meretricious gaudiness of the Church of Rome.

Now we want to consider the relationship of the developing Anglican Church to its culture. The Elizabethan Settlement presupposed that membership in the Church of England was identical with a citizen's membership in the nation: a citizen is a churchgoer, and a churchgoer is a citizen under another aspect. One exception was the Roman Catholic minority, who were regarded as traitors not only because their religion was deemed unsound, but also because they owed allegiance to a dangerous foreign power, the Roman papacy. The other exception was the Puritans, who dissented from the national church and were regarded as non-citizens, though what they prayed for was not merely the freedom to be themselves, but the freedom to dominate the national church as well. The Puritans shared with the Anglicans their belief that there was but one national community identical with the national church; however, they had different views of what the religion of the national church should be.

In his *Laws of Ecclesiastical Polity*, Hooker certainly identified citizenship and churchmanship. For example, when it was alleged that the monarch should not interfere in the affairs of the church, Hooker answered that the monarch through Parliament cared for the welfare of all citizens—cared for their bodies by just and wise legislation, and cared for their immortal souls by safeguarding and overseeing a church that would nourish them spiritually.

Through the centuries, this identity of church and nation in England came to be weakened through a number of causes. One was the emergence of strong religious groups outside of the national Anglican Church, while a second was the growing enfranchisement of members of these other groups, enabling them to become lawful citizens. A third factor, which emerged with the Oxford Movement, was the growing belief among church members that the church is a divine society, a part of the One Holy Catholic and Apostolic Church, neither to be identified with a nation nor subject to a national state.

Let us examine these three factors briefly. First, the splitting away of a large element of the Christian community was precipitated by the Stuart kings, Charles I and Charles II, who combined their strong Anglican loyalty with a will to persecute religious dissenters. This policy resulted in a division in the land between the monarchy, the aristocracy, and the Anglican clergy on the one side, and Parliament, the growing forces for democracy, and the Puritans on the other side. That clash was accentuated by some of the actions of Archbishop Laud, and eventually led to the deposition and execution of King Charles I. There followed the interlude of the Puritan Commonwealth, during which the Puritans took over the parish churches, expelled all the bishops, and allowed Puritan ministers to occupy the holy table and the pulpit.

The circle was completed by the restoration of Anglicanism and the monarchy in 1660. In that year, King Charles II attempted a rapprochement with the Puritans through a revision of the Prayer Book and the making of a new settlement. Since the 1662 Prayer Book was a bit more strongly Anglican than had been the Elizabethan Prayer Book, however, rapprochment was out of the question. A substantial body of Puritans made an exodus from the parishes, the pulpits, the rectories, and the church. They were allowed to keep their chapels (their places of worship), their religious practices, and their employments, but were denied full citizenship.

Thus there came about a major division in English religious and national life, one that used to be summarized under the heading of "Church and Chapel." "Church" referred to Anglicanism, usually conservative in politics, while "chapel" meant Puritan Nonconformist—that is, Presbyterian, Congregationalist, or Baptist—and eventually politically liberal. The subsequent religious life of England has been characterized by these groupings. Today we recognize that Puritanism contained some of the glories of Anglo-Saxon Christianity, and indeed of all Christianity. John Bunyan's *Pilgrim's Progress* and Richard Baxter's *The Reformed Pastor*, for example, are classical works of spirituality and pastoral theology. Above all, Puritan spirituality has produced great hymns, such as Isaac Watts' "When I survey the wondrous cross on which the Prince of Glory died."[3]

A further estrangement came about later in the eighteenth century, one perhaps even more tragic than the earlier division between church and chapel. This was, of course, the Methodist separation. John Wesley and his brother Charles were Anglicans and desired to continue in the Anglican Church, but they longed to see the Church of England renewed with a Christian mission to all the people. There is no doubt of the essential Anglicanism of the Wesleys themselves. The early Methodists had a daily Eucharist, and a reading of Charles Wesley's eucharistic hymns reveals similarities with Tractarian eucharistic hymns by William Bright and John Mason Neale.[4]

The cause of this sad separation was essentially twofold. First, the Methodist practice of itinerant evangelism, going here and everywhere, and entering parishes without the rector's leave under the urgency of preaching the Gospel, very much cut across the rather polite Anglican way of doing things. The second *casus belli* was the Wesleyan practice of presbyters' exercising the episcopal function of ordaining clergy to minister on this side of the Atlantic.

Whatever the causes, Methodism, which began as a renewal movement within the national church, separated and was later drawn into the general orbit of Nonconformity—dissenting Christianity in England. The result was the existence of a large Christian element outside the national church.

Later history witnessed the gradual enfranchisement of dissenting bodies, including Jews and Roman Catholics. The crown of the entire process was the admission of non-Anglicans to degree programs at Oxford and Cambridge. Prior to that, it would have been impossible to graduate from either university without signing the *Thirty-Nine Articles*, which at the time meant a declaration of assent to Anglican doctrine. Thus the identification of Christianity, national church, and citizenship came to be progressively dissolved.

Another important development was a growing catholic consciousness, whereby church members were unwilling to see themselves as just the organ of a national religion, but preferred to see themselves as representing the One Holy Catholic and Apostolic Church of Christ. The movement that powerfully revived this catholic church consciousness was, of course, the Oxford Movement, also known as the Tractarian Movement, which I will discuss in more detail in the next lecture. In the early days of the Oxford Movement, both Edward Pusey and John Henry Newman said they were cheered by the phenomenon of American Episcopalianism, particularly an episcopally-led church life that was neither dependent on nor subject to the state. This growing sense of the church led to its increasing autonomy in England, an autonomy that developed in several stages.

One important development took place in the year 1920 with the creation of the Church Assembly of bishops, clergy, and laity, a body that was empowered to legislate on church matters and take that legislation directly to the crown for assent without having to go through parliamentary deliberation. The climax of that process came in 1974 with the passage of "The Worship and Doctrine Measure," which gives to the General Synod of the Church of England the power to control its own liturgies and doctrines. According to this measure, the church may devise any new liturgies, new forms of worship, for any length of time, temporary or permanent, without those forms having to be approved by Parliament.

In spite of all these changes I have been describing, however, the monarch in England still has the title held by the first Queen Elizabeth, that of "Supreme Governor of the Church of England." Her powers as supreme governor are considerably less, of course, but they do exist. Church legislation is, for the most part, included in "the law of the land," and so goes out to the sovereign for signature. The queen still nominates the bishops, but she now does so on the recommendation of a commission of fifteen bishops, clergy, and lay-people; the role of the monarch as the supreme gover-nor is being considerably minimized. Another important factor in this continuing relationship is the coronation of the sovereign by the Archbishop of Canterbury. At her coronation, Queen Elizabeth II promised to be a loyal communicant of the Anglican Church, and to disallow the jurisdiction of the Bishop of Rome in the country.

Related to these developments is the fact that during previous centuries the Congregationalists, Presbyterians, and Baptists—the bodies that split off in the 1662 schism—had been very hostile to the link with the state and wished to have nothing to do with it. At the present time, however, it is fair to say that the Nonconformist bodies in England, desiring unity with the Church of England as much as the Church of England desires unity with them, would be quite willing to have a united church in relationship with the monarch—provided autonomy was preserved in the choice of their chief ministers and pastors, as well as in matters of their worship and doctrine.

This completes a rapid sketch and picture of the An-glican *via media* through many centuries on my side of the Atlantic Ocean.

Now, what about *your* side of the Atlantic? It is well for us to grasp the points of similarity and the points of contrast. Briefly, the contrast adds up to this: in England an Episcopalian establishment came into being, with other Christian bodies gradually coming to exist in revolt from it. In America, however, there exists a dominant, largely democratic, and Puritan style of religion, with the Episcopal Church compelled to fight for its identity. I believe that contrast ac-counts for a good deal in the ups and downs of history, as well as teaching us something about the relation between the Anglican tradition and the diversities of culture.

Well, you know your own history and you would not thank me for telling it all over again, but you might just be amused to hear what someone coming from the other side of the sea notices about it. One thing I have noticed is the fact that the Anglicans in Virginia were very good Elizabethan gentlemen. Here is a description of Anglicans in Virginia at worship, a very moving account indeed:

> When I first went to Virginia I well remember, we hung an awning (which is an old sail) to three or four trees, to shadow us from the sun and our walls were rails of wood and our seats were unhewed trees, till we cut planks, our pulpit was a bar of wood nailed to two neighboring trees, in foul weather we shifted into an old rotten tent, for we had few better and this came by way of adventure to do. This was our church till we built a homely thing like a barn and we had daily Common prayer, morning and evening. Every Sunday two sermons and every three months the Holy Communion, till our minister died. But, our prayers daily, with a homily on Sundays, we continued for years after, till more preachers came.[5]

That is a lovely picture, Elizabethan *via media*. There they are faithfully using the Book of Common Prayer, faithfully devoted to Morning and Evening Prayer and to Holy Communion—it was not held very frequently, but treated with very great devotion when it was. When their minister disappears, instead of electing one of their own number to be minister (as was happening in other parts of the country—upon my word, it was!), they did without until another minister came. Of course, they believed that the selection of ministers required the services of a bishop to consecrate them. That was the glory and the problem of it.

Massachusetts was a very different story from Virginia. Massachusetts Christians were largely exiles from what they held to be English tyranny and the settlement of Charles II. They were anxious to be free to run a church in their own way, and to enjoy on this side of the Atlantic some of the practices of the Commonwealth interlude in England. They regarded themselves as an establishment, though not all of them liked their presbyterian polity. It was in that atmosphere that Episcopalians—and there were some—found themselves under very great pressure to conform to the Puritan religion around them. Therefore, on this side of the ocean, we witness the paradox of an Episcopal Church that found it very difficult to locate bishops (partly because it did not know where to find them) and would have been a bit suspicious of bishops even if they had found them, because of the strong democratic strain in their religion. Yet the religion of the Prayer Book did continue, and where Prayer Book religion is found, the ministry of bishops as well as priests is still necessary.

Where were the bishops to be found after the War of Independence? Not in England, because there it was illegal to consecrate a bishop who would not take the oath of allegiance and obedience to the English crown. Thus the consecration of American bishops at that stage was impossible. Hence American Episcopalians, eager to have bishops, sent Samuel Seabury to Scotland where there was an episcopate of a free kind, not under the English establishment. His consecration as bishop was a great step forward.[6]

Meanwhile, England had woken up to the new situation, and in 1787 Parliament made it lawful to consecrate bishops without requiring them to take the oath of allegiance to the crown, since it was understood they would be functioning overseas in other countries and other parts of the world. This made possible the consecration of American bishops in England, and a number were consecrated by the Archbishop of Canterbury in his chapel of Lambeth, near the tomb of Matthew Parker. Only two years later, in 1789, the Episcopal Church set up its own constitution and synodical government, and its own procedure for the election and consecration of bishops. Apparently the Anglican tradition is able to cope with extremely diverse cultural traditions, for if it can cope with cultural traditions as diverse as the two we have been thinking about, it is likely to be able to cope with a greater variety still.

I mentioned that the early Tractarians recognized the importance of Episcopalianism in America in demonstrating that Anglicanism was not, in essence, merely a department of the state, but a spiritual body, a true and autonomous part of the Church of Christ. Both Pusey and Newman wrote of how greatly they were encouraged by this phenomenon of the Episcopal Church in America. But they also had certain reservations, and both were very critical of the American church on two counts. First, Pusey and Newman criticized the American bishops for suppressing the use of the Athanasian Creed in public worship. That was something the Tractarians felt very strongly about; they felt it to be a diminution of the evidence of orthodoxy. In the second place, they thought that in the American church the bishops were subject to the laity and that this subjection resulted in a secularization of the church. "The Americans boast that their church is not, like ours, enslaved to the civil power," wrote Newman. "True, not to the civil power by name and in form, but to the laity. And in a democracy, what is that but civil power in another shape?"[7]

For there is more than one way in which secular political influence can infect a church. A church can be politically affected by its link with a monarchy and an aristocracy, but it can also be politically affected by its own democratic procedures if they resemble too closely those of the secular state.

We have observed two very different cultural-political settings for Anglicanism, and Anglicanism functioning strongly in both of them. Indeed, the Anglican Communion does not depend upon political and cultural settings because it is able to move into so many. In both the last century and the present one, the Anglican Church has moved into all continents and among many different races and nationalities, so that Anglo-Saxons are now only a minority within the total Anglican population of the world. Of course, cultural bonds are real bonds, while theological bonds can be cultural bonds, too. Because of the great cultural diversity in the Anglican Communion, its future unity, coherence, integrity, and vigorous mission to the world will not depend upon cultural forces, but is going to rely upon the heritage of spirituality, theological principle, and tradition. The Anglican Communion will fulfill this mission if it realizes that it has within itself spiritual treasures that are able to transcend cultural differences and may even be able to unite them.

What is the true relationship between Christianity and the world's cultures? It is possible for the church to merge itself with the world's cultures, to be so identified with them as to lose the power of criticizing them and healing them. It is possible for the Christian church, on the contrary, to remain aloof from the world's diverse cultures in its own quest for spiritual purity and integrity, and to make no impact upon them at all. Those are obviously both unsatisfactory stances. Is it not the true calling of the church to identify itself with all that is good in culture, in such a way as to be able to influence it—but influence it because the church represents a spirituality that transcends the barriers of time and place?

Anglo-Catholicism and the Oxford Movement

EARLY IN THE nineteenth century, the Anglican Church both in England and in America was facing an immense new state of things in the world, beginning with the Industrial Revolution and, not very long after that, a revolution in the sciences. Meanwhile Americans were about to face a tremendous new influx in population due to immigration, and considerable spreading of its nationality and culture westward to the frontier.

In England the important question was: what *is* the Church of England? Clear to all was the fact that the Church of Englican was a historic institution linked with both the monarchy and the Tory party, and possessing considerable wealth. This was a time when the inequitable distribution of wealth was beginning to trouble social consciences, particularly in the wake of the French Revolution. On the surface, in terms of custom and polity, it was not difficult to say what the Church of England was. Still, in the deeper matters of faith, belief, and future calling, what was the Church of England?

Two very different answers were proposed at a time when, as an institution, the church was facing hostility from a number of quarters. One answer was that given by the rising school of Latitudinarians, later to be called Liberals, who answered that the Church of

England is the national church of this country, and ideally the church of all the people. Therefore let it unite all the Christians in the land under its umbrella, and as times are changing, the fewer dogmas and the more comprehensiveness the better. The Liberals' desire was for a multi-comprehensive liberal church under the aegis of the crown.

The most famous exponent of this view was Thomas Arnold,[1] headmaster of Rugby School and a professor of history at Oxford. In a later phase, this point of view was also shared by Dean Stanley,[2] the Dean of Westminster in the middle of the century. Had the Church of England simply adopted the Liberal agenda it would probably have been fatal, but that was the Liberals' answer at the time.

The High Church answer was quite different. No, they said, the Church of England is the representative of a divine supernatural society on English soil. That was the response of those who were soon to be called the Tractarians, as well as by the old High Church element in the Church of England, made up of a number of "high and dry" priests and lay people. Some of these were very faithful and simply continuing an old tradition, linking their church practice with nostalgia for the monarchy. But in the context of the Church of England as representative of the One Holy Catholic, and Apostolic Church, the Tractarians were not being merely archaic. They were looking back—to the Caroline divines and the ancient Fathers of the church—but also looking up, because the church was to them a supernatural society, the body on earth of the risen Jesus, who through the Holy Spirit, sanctifies men and women and makes saints. It was the supernatural liveliness of the Tractarians that made their appeal to the One Holy Catholic Church anything but high and dry, and anything but a mere archaism.

Who were these Tractarians? There was John Keble, the son of a High Church country rector. He represented the older piety, and he was a learned man, a very faithful country pastor and poet. Through his poetry, *The Christian Year*, and *Lyra Innocentium*, Keble helped bring a romantic poetic flavor into the movement and give it a contemporary air, since it was linked with the romantic revival that was taking place both in England and throughout the Continent.[3]

Edward Bouverie Pusey was a contemporary of Keble's in the movement. Becoming Professor of Hebrew at Oxford at a very young age, he was a man immensely learned in the Church Fathers, as well as in Hebrew studies. Pusey had a reputation for austerity; he was sadly austere in both his piety and his self-discipline, though he always had about him a deep, otherworldly kind of joy. Pusey's massive learning all went into controversy, where he argued and fought with great batteries of ammunition drawn from earlier Anglican divines and the Fathers. His participation in the movement meant that the tracts, instead of being exciting little pamphlets, were massive treatises, and if you look at a volume of the tracts you can see how the Pusey influence rather changed their character.

Finally, there was John Henry Newman.[4] He was a bit different from the other two in that he had a good deal less church background. Newman had always been religious. He experienced a deep, evangelical-style conversion as a teenager, and he found in the spirituality of Keble and Pusey and their colleagues a spirituality that did not supercede, but fulfilled and enriched his youthful experience of conversion. I think that without question Newman was the genius of the Oxford Movement, and his sermons in the pulpit of St. Mary's, Oxford, where he was vicar, are probably the most powerful exposition of all the main themes of the movement.[5]

So these men and a few others felt a call to revive both a belief in the Holy Catholic Church as truly describing the Church of England and the supernatural call to holiness which gives that belief its meaning. Keble's great book of poems, *The Christian Year*, was published in 1827. The tracts began appearing in 1833, and the first tract, by John Henry Newman, was only four pages long. Its theme is this: What are we clergy for? We are not here to be nice, kind gentlemen in our parishes, but to represent an apostolic commission, starting from the apostles themselves and carried down to us through their successors the bishops. Newman appeals to his fellow clergy to stir up the grace of ordination that is in them, an appeal characteristic of the Oxford Movement in its incisiveness, clericalism, and narrow focus upon the apostolic commission. He treated the line of apostolic succession carried down by consecration and ordination as if that were the sole lifeline the church depended on, and he believed that reviving the clergy would revive the whole church.[6]

The teaching of the Oxford Movement was derived partly from Newman's sermons at St. Mary's, Oxford, partly from the tracts, partly from a few country parishes where similar work was going on, and partly from Pusey's growing ministry in Oxford as a teacher, counselor, and confessor. The teaching centered on the Holy Catholic Church, which was not just an institution that went back a very long way, but really meant the representation on earth of a church that essentially belongs to heaven. The church includes saints in heaven as well as its representatives on earth, because the heart of the church is the living Christ himself. I quote from one of Newman's parochial sermons:

We may form a clearer notion...of the one Catholic Church which is in all lands. Properly it is not on earth, except so far as heaven can be said to be on earth, or the dead are still with us. It is not on earth, except in such sense as Christ or His Spirit are on earth....The Ministry and Sacraments, the bodily presence of Bishop and people, are given us as keys and spells, by which we bring ourselves into the presence of the great company of Saints; they are as much as this, but they are no more; they are not identical with that company; they are but the outskirts of it; they are but the porches to the pool of Bethesda, entrances into that which is indivisible and one. Baptism admits, not into a mere visible society, varying with the country in which it is administered, Roman here, and Greek there, and English there, but *through* the English, *or* the Greek, *or* the Roman porch into the invisible company of elect souls, which is independent of time and place...[And] when we are called to do battle for the Lord, what are we who are seen but mere outposts, the advanced guard of a mighty host, ourselves few in number and despicable, but bold beyond our numbers, because supported by chariots of fire and horses of fire round about the Mountain of the Lord of Hosts under which we stand?[6]

And on that mountain, you see, are the saints of every age. The church can be described both as a historical institution, with a pedigree from the past, and also as the contemporary supernatural action of the living Christ through the sacraments, the Word, and the existence of the people of God on earth.

Let me quote another sermon of Newman, one that is very moving indeed. Its title is "Worship, a Preparation for Christ's Coming," and shows that in their doctrine of the church the Tractarians were not merely looking back, nor only to the contempory supernatural life, but—in the authentic spirit of New Testament es-

chatology—towards the future, towards the *parousia*,
towards the coming of Christ. Here Newman describes
the sacramental actions of the church not only as
things visible and tangible, but also as acts of the un-
seen living Christ to prepare us for his coming:

> At times we seem to catch a glimpse of a Form
> which we shall hereafter see face to face. We ap-
> proach, and in spite of the darkness, our hands, or
> our head, or our brow, or our lips become, as it
> were, sensible of the contact of something more
> than earthly. We know not where we are, but we
> have been bathing in water, and a voice tells us
> that it is blood. Or we have a mark signed upon our
> foreheads, and it spake of Calvary. Or we recollect a
> hand laid upon our heads, and surely it had the
> print of nails in it, and resembled His who with a
> touch gave sight to the blind and raised the dead.
> Or we have been eating and drinking; and it was
> not a dream surely, that One fed us from His
> wounded side, and renewed our nature by the
> heavenly meat He gave.[7]

That was the spirit of Tractarian ecclesiology. It
evoked a great deal of controversy, because it involved
beliefs that were foreign to the Evangelicals of the
time, foreign to the rising and still immature Liberals
of the time, and, indeed, foreign to the bulk of the
episcopate.

What were these foreign elements? "Foreign," that
is, in the sense of "unfamiliar" to the Church of England? First, there was the Tractarians' teaching about
baptism and baptismal regeneration. That was
strongly emphasized, and the classic document is the
tract on baptism by Pusey, which comes quite early in
Tracts for the Times.[8] Pusey taught that in baptism,
including the baptism of infants, all people—men,
women, and children—are really "born again." They
are brought into a new ontological state, a new onto-

logical relation to God and Christ, and become genuine parts of God's new creation.

The Evangelicals objected that such a teaching made conversion identical with regeneration. That was not so in the Tractarian thesis, where this new status and new membership had to be responded to, and where conversion could be a process sometimes slow and gradual, in which the baptized laid upon themselves the privileges of baptism. Yet so strong was their emphasis upon what was objectively wrought in baptism, that the Tractarians were distinguished by a particular horror of post-baptismal sin; for them it was the terrible, almost unspeakable thing. The world at large sins, so why be shocked or surprised if pagans sin? But for baptized Christians to sin is a contradiction of what they truly and essentially are.

It was that emphasis upon the horror of post-baptismal sin that gave the note to Tractarian morality. Their intense call for holiness derived from the belief that the existence of sin in a Christian at all is just unspeakable. In that context, therefore, the sacrament of penance became prominent as God's remedy for those who fall into post-baptismal sin. That, in its sacramentalism and in its moralism, was very characteristic of the Tractarians. Of course it was very foreign to the easy-going style of the Broad church types as well as to Evangelical teaching, which made personal conversion and not necessarily baptism the starting point of Christian response to our Lord.

Another controversial point was the Holy Eucharist. The Tractarians revived some very realistic language about the presence of Christ in the Eucharist. It was a revival that had a good deal of support from the seventeenth-century Anglican divines and, more importantly, from the church fathers, although their borrowings from the latter were rather indiscriminate. This language had a strong emphasis upon the literalness of the Lord's words, "This is my body....This is my blood." Although they repudiated any notion of carnal or physical presence, and insisted that the presence of Christ was after a spiritual and heavenly manner, they still believed it was objectively *there* in and through the consecrated gifts of bread and wine. The classic bits of teaching about this are Keble's short work *On Eucharistical Adoration,* and the sermon of Pusey entitled "The Holy Eucharist, a Comfort to the Penitent."[9]

This teaching on the Eucharist, combined with their teaching on baptism and its corollary, the need for the sacrament of penance—indeed, not only taught but carried out in Pusey's ministrations,[10]—all these were foreign to the times. The controversies they engendered ran their course and were the subject of an immense volume of preaching and counterpreaching and letters and quotations and arguments and so forth. While Pusey carried on most of the controversy, Keble supplied the humble religious spirit and Newman the imaginative preaching of a poetic and indeed very biblical kind.

Now, one theological issue of much importance became prominent at this time and we need to explore it a little more. It was the doctrine of justification. And to see what it was they were arguing about we have to step right back to Martin Luther and his interpretation of St. Paul. I shall attempt to be brief without misrepresenting the issues. Martin Luther, horrified by the contemporary idea that salvation could be won by merit or good works, proclaimed that justification is by faith alone. How does a person become right with God? How does a person become accepted? Not through earning it by works, nor as a reward for works, but by receiving faith. So that although sinful and morally feeble, someone may, on the basis of that act of faith, be accepted by God and be *simul justus et peccator.*

Inevitably, people being the way they are, it was possible for the trend against justification by works to lead on to a movement for no works at all, with the danger of sheer antinomianism right around the corner. In fairness to Martin Luther, one must insist that for him, the life of justification by faith was a life of relationship to God in Christ, of such a kind that the Holy Spirit did the rest in the fruit of good works. In the preface to his commentary on Romans, his chief work on the subject, Luther said this:

> Faith is a divine work in us, through which we are changed and regenerated by God....Oh, it is a living, busy, active, powerful thing, faith, so it is impossible for it not to do good continually. It never asks whether good works are to be done; it has done them before there is time to ask the question, and it is doing them always.

There is no doubt that for Luther, the status of faith led on through the power of the Spirit to sanctification and to good works. Nonetheless, Luther had to keep drumming the anti-salvation-by-works drum. Righteousness is imputed by God; it is assigned, not earned or deserved. In a letter to Melancthon Luther used the famous phrase, *"Esto peccator et pecca fortiter...."*

> Be a sinner and sin bravely, but more bravely have faith in Christ...because that which we have known suffices...the Lamb of God who takes away the sins of the world; and from this sin will not tear us away, even though we fornicate or commit murder a thousand, thousand times in one day.[13]

It is on that rhetorical passage that allegations that Luther himself espoused antinomianism are largely based. To me it seems odd that the commentators on this do not think that Luther was very likely pulling Melancthon's leg; I think it more than likely that he was, especially as the account suggests that Melancthon, a rather solemn person, had the kind of leg that sometimes needed to be pulled!

In reaction to the supposed antinomianism of Luther, for his supposed neglect of sanctification, as distinct from the initial act of justification, the tendency in the Roman Catholic Church was to identify justification with sanctification. I think it fair to say that the Council of Trent, in its treatment of the subject, equated justification with being made righteous by the Holy Spirit—the grace is God's, but faith comes from the recipient. The actual sanctification and justification are fused together.

Now, the Tractarians were very, very ignorant of Luther's theology, and indeed we Anglicans have generally been ignorant of Luther's theology, too. I remember a great shock when a Lutheran professor from Germany visited one of our seminaries in England, and asked the dean of the seminary if the students read Luther in the original German or in an English translation—and of course the poor dean and his students would have read neither. The Tractarians were rather ignorant of Luther, but much aware of a rather debased kind of *solifidianism* that existed in the later generations in Evangelicals in England, after the real force of that movement had spent itself. The Tractarians followed the line that justification must be identified with sanctification, that is, justification means actually being made righteous. That was the teaching of Pusey in several sermons, as well as Newman's in a very prominent work, *Lectures on Justification*.

Let me say a word about that book. First off, I think it is certainly unfair as a critique of Luther. It may also be unfair as a critique of contemporary Evangelicalism, though there was much in contemporary Evangelicalism that lent itself to that kind of criticism. But *Lectures on Justification* contains the most moving passages you will ever read about the justified life being a life in Christ informed by the Holy Spirit, a life that is loving and fruitful. One passage I want to quote is striking and important for its application to many different concepts. Newman protests against those who make the doctrine of "justification by faith" itself an object of faith, so that instead of believing in Christ who justifies, one believes in the doctrine. One makes the doctrine a substitute for believing in the Christ who justifies. In making this criticism, Newman uses this language:

> True faith is what may be called colourless, like air or water; it is but the medium through which the soul sees Christ; and the soul as little rests on it and contemplates it, as the eye can see the air. When, then, men are bent on holding [justification by faith] in their hands, curiously inspecting, analyzing, and so aiming at it, they are obliged to colour and thicken it, that it may be seen and touched. That is, they substitute for it something or other, a feeling, notion, sentiment, conviction, an act of reason, which they hang over, and dote upon. They rather aim at experiences (as they are called) within them, than at Him that is without them....So it is with faith and other Christian graces....As God's grace elicits our faith, so His holiness stirs our fear, and His glory kindles our love. Others may say of us "here is faith," and "there is conscientiousness," and "there is love;" but we can only say, "this is God's grace," and "that is His holiness," and "that is His glory."[11]

That passage, very moving, seems to me to be very penetrating as well, because it is an implied criticism of every kind of Christian piety that dwells upon the medium of grace and salvation, rather than upon he who gives it. Believing in the "real presence of Christ," rather than believing in the Christ whose presence it is. Believing in a thing call "salvation," rather than believing in God in Christ the Savior. Believing in the dogma of the Trinity, rather than rejoicing in the life of the threefold God, a life that comes to us, and so on. Indeed, Newman's words seem to be a salutary protest against every form of religiosity—or shall we call it "spikiness"—that worships the symbol rather than He whose symbols these are in giving His very life to human souls.

Now, there was quite a problem concerning Newman. The Oxford Movement evoked considerable hostility from Evangelicals, from Liberals, from academics, from bishops, and from people in general who smelled "popery" simply because they knew no better. And it is here that we turn to the particular problem of Newman. Newman had been, I believe, the most powerful exponent of the beliefs he shared with all his colleagues. But, in a sense he was not quite of it, that is, he had not quite gotten historic Anglicanism into his bones in the way that the others had, and he came to it rather as one who is fulfilling deep personal needs of his own.

Besides the *Lectures on Justification*, Newman wrote a very powerful exposition of the principles of the movement, a work called *The Prophetical Office of the Church*, first published in 1837. (When it was republished later in his life it had the title *The Via Media: The Prophetical Office of the Church*.) This is an exposition of the Anglican position along these lines. He begins with a compelling description of the primitive church in its life of simplicity and holiness, and then asks, "What is there in the modern world that is identical with and representative of that way of life?" He rejects the Church of Rome because the papacy and a number of other Roman Catholic doctrines were simply not found in the primitive church. (Newman's anti-Romanism at that stage was very strong indeed.) What is there, then, in the contemporary world that has continuity and identity with the pure church of antiquity? For continuity, the Anglican Church is his answer, for he sees a real continuity in belief, in sacramental order, and in the supernatural life between the Anglican Church in principle and the primitive church. Thus Newman is happy in the Anglican *via media*.

Yet perhaps not quite happy, because he does speak about this Anglican identity with the primitive church as something still needing to be realized by the recovery of certain doctrines, rather than something that already exists. And so even in this superb exposition of the Anglican *via media*, we can see just the trace of a haunting specter of skepticism—because the Anglican Church in practice, with so many tiresome things about it, is falling short of that vocation in which its identity should lie. That is part of the Newman problem.

Another aspect of the Newman problem came to a head in the last of the *Tracts*, the tract called *Tract Ninety*, which was Newman's treatment of the *Thirty-Nine Articles of Religion*. There Newman argued that the more controversial of the articles attacked popular Roman Catholic doctrine of the later middle ages, and not the doctrines of the Council of Trent, because the *Articles* were written before the Council of Trent decreed about those matters. The *Articles* attacked the corrupt notions of purgatory and veneration of the saints in the later middle ages. Similarly, in Article Twenty-Three on transubstantiation, Newman claimed that in objecting to transubstantiation it did not reject the refined and spiritualized notion later

put out in the Council of Trent, but the carnal concepts of transubstantiation. With Article Thirty-One,
"The Sacrifices of the Masses," Newman maintains
that what was under attack was not the kind of doctrine promulgated by Trent. Rather, as the plural
form "sacrifices of the masses" suggests, it objected to
the idea that the sacrifice of Calvary could be actually
repeated in the mass, while repetitions in further
masses could win salvation, assist souls, and also,
coincidentally, help to give ample remuneration to the
priests who were paid by the number of the masses
they said.

This thesis of Newman about the *Thirty Nine Articles* sounded at the time very novel indeed, though it
had been heard before, and it did cause a great shock
among those who said, "There we go! We always told
you the Tractarians were heading towards Rome, and
now they are trying to justify Roman Catholic doctrine by a kind of rather dishonest use of the *Articles
of Religion*." (I would say that to a large extent Newman's thesis about the *Articles* has come to be ap-
plauded and approved not only by Anglo-Catholics,
but also by fairminded students of history—both the
history of the sixteenth century and the history of the
Articles themselves. But that Newman should claim
this to any extent at all, you see, did cause a great
sense of scandal.) The ensuing controversy and subsequent condemnation of Newman's *Tract Ninety* by
the university and many of the bishops, heightened
his sense of loneliness and sensitivity, leading him to
wonder, "Am I in the True Church at all?" In theory,
yes—but in fact, is this church really recovering the
vocation to be its own true self?"

The final crisis in Newman's mind came in the
course of his study of Christian antiquity. He was always studying the ancient church, and indeed he was
delighted to see the doctrinal identity between the an-

cient church of the Fathers and the Anglican Church as he understood it. But a question began to pose itself: "Where is this ancient church to be found? For surely there is but one Holy Catholic Church, and you are either in it or outside it. And because the Church is established to be one, and is supernaturally one, possessing the one Spirit of Christ, it cannot be divided. So either you are in it or out of it." That is how the question posed itself. Newman believed strongly in the line of thought that said, "Here is a true primitive faith and the Roman Catholics have not kept it." However, that view came to be superceded in his heart and mind by another line of reasoning: "There can be but one true Catholic Church, and I seem to be outside it."

In his reading of the Fathers, and particularly the story of St. Augustine and the Donatists, and the story of Chalcedon and the Monophysites, Newman was haunted by the words, *Securus judicat orbis terrarum*: ("The world judges safely.")[12] Of himself he said, while reading the history of the fifth century dispute concerning Eutyches and the one-nature heresy, that like most of the bishops who wished compromise against Rome, "I saw my face in that mirror, and I was a Monophysite.[13] Of course Newman did not believe their doctrines, but his thinking was obsessed with the question of one true church, which could not be divided. If you were not in it, you were outside it.

It was that crisis of belief that led to Newman's final tragedy. And it was a tragedy. On October 8, 1845, he wrote to a friend, "Tonight I am expecting Father Dominic, the Passionist, and I mean to ask him for admission to the one fold of Christ."

How was Newman to justify the position he was adopting in view of his great allegiance to the faith and the church of antiquity? He justified it by the publication of a book on which he had already been working before he was converted, a book called *An Essay on the Development of Christian Doctrine.*[14] His thesis was this: you do not see the later Roman doctrines, either papacy or mariology, in the primitive church, yet hidden in the primitive church there were seeds that were later to grow into what the Church of Rome subsequently became.

But there is development and there is development. In the rest of these lectures, other ideas of development will be assessed. In the next lecture we will give a little more thought to the problem of ecclesiology, both for Newman, who left, and for those who stayed. For many did stay, and here is a glimpse into why some of them stayed—a random description from a letter written by a friend of John Keble's, describing his life:

> I sent the same to John Keble, a friend who is in great distress about faith and many controversies. He lived with John Keble for a month or two. John Keble said no word of controversy, but lived. And my friend's faith was restored and his place in the Anglican Church was restored.

And it is in those words, "but lived," that the crisis was overcome and we are now, you and I, where we are.

After the Tractarians

THE OXFORD MOVEMENT initiated a deep spiritual and intellectual revival in the Anglican Church. I would allude in passing to an aspect of that revival that I find very interesting and moving—the renaissance of religious community life. The first religious order for men, founded a bit later on, was the community known as the "Cowley Fathers," the Society of St. John the Evangelist.[1] Three men took vows in that order in 1866, two Englishmen, Richard Meux Benson and Simeon Wilberforce O'Neil, and an American, Charles Grafton.[2] It is particularly good to remember that one of the three initial "Cowley Fathers" was an American priest. Charles Grafton subsequently returned to America, where he played a very notable part as a Christian teacher, and I will mention him once or twice in these lectures for the fascination of seeing this interplay between our two countries.

Now, with their powerful revival of theology and spirituality, the Tractarians appear in the longer perspective of history to have had a number of weaknesses and defects, weaknesses from which later Anglican theology had to emerge. First, in their theology the Tractarians were prescientific—the scientific critical study of the Bible came after their time. Nor were they open to allowing the scientific revolution to affect their understanding of theology; the Tractarians were rigidly conservative in scriptural literalism and in matters of history. Furthermore, they were undiscriminating even in their study and use of the Fathers, missing a number of variations of light and shade, and presenting Christian antiquity in a rather unscientifically uniform way.

In subsequent decades, however, the heirs of the Tractarians began to be sensitive to the scientific revolution, and they made adjustments between their theology and the new scientific understanding of the world. Indeed, the Tractarians themselves made one or two significant steps in that direction. As a very old man, Edward Pusey preached a sermon called "Unscience, Not Science, the Enemy of the Faith,"[3] in which he discussed the Darwinian theory of evolution that was beginning to make a stir. People assumed that he was going to denounce it wholeheartedly, but he did not. Pusey said in that sermon—which is well worth reading—that the creation of the world might have happened in the kind of way that Darwin's *The Origin of the Species* describes, with one proviso. He felt it to be inconceivable that the human soul should be part of the evolutionary process. But provided that the human soul is a special creation, he did not think that the evolutionary account of creation was necessarily going to be wrong or harmful. Spare the human soul, Pusey said. He did not fear science, but "unscience"—and by that he meant the application of the theory of evolution to matters like the human soul, of which it knew nothing. That is a remarkable episode in the life of that very learned, very conservative man.

Earlier I mentioned Charles Grafton, who became the second bishop of Fond du Lac in the United States, in 1889. Bishop Grafton was know as an ardent disciple of Pusey and Liddon and an exponent of Tractarian Christianity, yet we find him saying in his autobiography, *A Journey Godward*:

To deny what is called the Darwinian theory, or the evolutionary process, is as unwise as to deny the truths of the world's...orbit about the sun....The discovery of the law of progress in the natural world...is in favor of the doctrine of the progressive development of man (in and through the incarnate Lord) into a final union with God, which secures sinlessness and eternal life...The larger [truth] is that God, in spite of man's sinfulness, came to forgive and lift him up into a higher degree of union. In the Incarnate One, creation advances to its completion.[4]

So there was that American, a devoted Tractarian, having a glimpse of that union of revelation and creation which was to mark a later phase of American catholic theology. But by and large the Tractarians were pre-scientific.

A second fault in Tractarian theology can also be detected. While the Holy Catholic Church was their great doctrine, they saw it in an institutional way that missed some of the biblical imagery in understanding the church. For instance, we do not find in the Tractarians an emphasis upon the union between the eucharistic Body and Christians themselves that figured so strongly, for example, in St. Augustine's teachings. Augustine had said, "If you then are the body and members of Christ, the mystery of your souls is laid upon the table of the Lord, the mystery of your souls you receive." That close union between the Body of Christ received by believers and the body that is made up of the faithful themselves was, I think, rather a later realization in the growing movement of Anglican theology. But the view is Augustinian, and if the Tractarians had known a little more about Martin Luther, they would have also realized that this aspect of the church was one that Martin Luther had himself very strongly revived.

Another biblical aspect of the church that the Tractarians do not seem to have emphasized is the image of the *ecclesia*, the new Israel, the People of God, the elect race. They thought of the unity of the church very much in institutional terms, using the imagery of the body in their own way, but we do find in St. Paul, 1 Peter, and in the very language of the *ecclesia* the thought that the church is the elect race, the people of God, those who share a spiritual rebirth. The unity of Christians is basically a unity of race. And if the unity of Christians is basically one of spiritual race through their common baptism, then its unity can continue in spite of organic divisions and quarrels (see 1 Corinthians 12:12ff and 1 Peter 2:9-10). Organic divisions and quarrels, furthermore, are wrong and need to be healed because they contradict that deep unity of the Christian fellowship of the People of God. Only later did Anglican theology recover the great significance of the church's image, the "People of God."

Now a third criticism must be made. The Tractarian view of the apostolic succession of the ministry was lopsided and out of context. From the first, *Tracts for the Times* spoke of the apostolic succession as if it were the principal test of the presence of the Holy Catholic Church, the thread on which everything else hung. They certainly used that kind of language, and brought a certain distortion into Anglican thinking that may not have wholly disappeared.

Now what is the truth of the matter? Let me try to put the truth of the matter as simply as possible. There are two erroneous views of the origins of church and ministry. One view says this: "Christ created an apostolic ministry, and on *that* alone the life of the church subsequently depended." That was one pole of the argument, and the other, equally erroneous, is this: "Christ created the church, and subsequently the church invented a ministry to suit it." It is rather like a club appointing a secretary, a treasurer, and so on.

What in fact did happen (and the evidence of the gospels, epistles, and other writings of the early church are pretty clear on this point) is that Christ created a church, and Christ created an apostolic ministry within it, with structural significance. And indeed the apostolic ministry does not exist in its own right apart from the created church, of which it is a part. Thus church and ministry have a great deal of interplay. I do not think the Tractarians got that quite right. Perhaps we have not yet got it right either, but if we are to do so, I am sure we have to grasp the creation of both apostolic ministry and church by Jesus, and the interrelationship of the two.[5]

Meanwhile, partly through their success, partly through their fervor, and partly through their limitations, the Tractarians were a divisive as well as a renewing force in Anglican history. Indeed, the nineteenth century was a time of conflict, a conflict between three sides of a triangle. The Tractarians had their novelties. The Evangelicals, who were still doing an immense amount of pastoral work, as well as evangelism both at home and overseas, were to begin (unfortunately) devoting some of their energies to combating the Tractarians. Then there were the Liberals, or Latitudinarians, searching for ways to learn about God and revelation within the burgeoning scientific revolution. For the Liberals it was very important to hold in balance the givenness of revelation and the novelty of exploration, and some did and some did not.

Now this period of conflict is familiar to many, and my task is merely to draw attention to certain characteristics of nineteenth-century Anglican theology. So let me refer to the significance of an Anglican of that century who stood somewhat outside those contemporary controversies and certainly did not fit any of the usual labels. This Anglican is Frederick Denison Maurice.[6]

Maurice had been brought up a Unitarian, but he became an ardent trinitarian believer, an Anglican, and a priest. He lived from 1805 to 1872. The offices he held were mostly pastoral preaching and parochial posts, though he was for a short time a professor at King's College, London (before he was expelled in 1853), and in the last few years of his life he was professor of moral philosophy at Cambridge. Maurice was little understood at the time, but had a great deal more influence after his death. In looking at his life, I think we can see three creative themes that are new and invigorating. I would call these themes the Kingdom of Christ, eternal life, and Christian Socialism, and each of them was for Maurice an intensely theological one.

First, the "Kingdom of Christ." It is a title of a book he published in 1838, so it was contemporary with the Tractarian movement. This book was an exposition of the church, with the full title *The Kingdom of Christ; or Hints to a Quaker concerning the Principle, Constitution, and Ordinances of the Catholic Church*. Now the difference between Maurice's method and the Tractarian method was this: the latter started with revelation and said, "Here is the revealed truth about the church"—and everyone who disagreed was, of course, in great error. Maurice's method was, rather, inductive. He took certain contemporary theological and ecclesiological positions, respected them very much for what they were, and sought to show that, good as they were, they missed the mark and were never fully realized because of their isolation. However, he noted that the things these positions tried to stand for would find their realization within the family of a universal society ordained and constituted by God.

For example, the Quaker to whom the book is addressed, this Quaker greatly values the inner light. But very often his conception of the inner light becomes secularized, or it is absorbed into a kind of broad—and not particularly Christian—mysticism. If the Quaker could only see that Christ is the light, and the light is realized in the common life of a family, a universal family, then the Quaker would find the thing he wants to stand for to be far more fully realized than he does at present.

Or consider the ardent Protestant who believes in justification by faith. By treating this doctrine in isolation from any other, it becomes a kind of shibboleth he worships. Would not this Protestant do better to find himself within the company of the redeemed, within the divine family of people of very different kinds of experience and language? There he would find that fulfillment of faith about which he cares so much.

Finally, even the Unitarian who cares so much about the unity of God—Maurice understands that, because he was himself a Unitarian in childhood. But what does unity mean? Unity does not mean the unity of a kind of bare digit. Unity means the richness of the united life, of an indwelling Father, Son, and Spirit, reflected in turn in the life of a human society that mirrors the Trinity in human life.

Here then is a simple account of Maurice's method. He meets people on their own ground and attempts to show that the Christian church, not as an *exclusive* institution but rather as an outreaching family, brings fulfillment of all these different aspirations which, though by themselves inadequate, do indeed have to be respected.

Now this was obviously a presentation different from the Tractarians' and indeed different from every dogmatic school. In putting forth this thesis, Maurice ran afoul of the rising school of Liberals because he emphasized so strongly the historic givenness of divine revelation and redemption. He also ran afoul of the Evangelicals because he was not able to use the kind of language that they were using, and last of all he ran afoul of the Tractarians. Why? Because while they were interested in affirming a society of the redeemed, standing over against a hostile world, Maurice himself was interested in affirming that the visible church was a sign that God had redeemed all humanity. The fact of redemption and the fact of the church, said Maurice, proclaims that Christ is the Lord of all people, and everyone is potentially within the Christian family already.

Maurice also emphasized the divine presence in everyone. Not infrequently he used the phrase, "Christ is in every man," a strong affirmation of the indwelling presence of the divine *logos* everywhere. And I think that he both annoyed the Tractarians and let them annoy him in the language he used about baptism. To the Tractarians, baptism meant bringing this child within the ark of salvation. Maurice believed that too, but for him the great thing about baptism was its proclamation that Christ has redeemed all children and that all children are potentially saved. He had his eye on its potential significance for all humanity, rather than on its immediate significance for those who accept it and are saved. And so we find Maurice using language like this (which could not have made him popular):

> I do not fancy that you will get much satisfaction from the Oxford Tracts, but I cannot tell. To me they are, for the most part, more unpleasant than I quite like to acknowledge to myself or others. Their

error, I think, consists in opposing to "the spirit of
the present age" the spirit of a former age, instead
of the ever-living and acting Spirit of God, of which
the spirit of each age (as it presents itself to those
living in it) is at once the adversary and the
parody.[7]

If Maurice's words were not popular with the
Tractarians, neither did he endear himself to the Liberals, as when he wrote, for example, that they had
succumbed to, "...the great disease of our time, that
we talk about God and about our religion, and do not
confess Him as a Living God; Himself the Redeemer of
men in His Son."[8] Thus Maurice laments the failure
of the Liberals to emphasize as strongly as he did
himself the givenness of divine revelation.

In relationship to the whole Victorian climate, nothing is more characteristic of Maurice than the contrast he made between religion and the living God. To
the intense religious temper of the last century in
England, and in America, too, for that matter, religion
and God had become more or less identified. So Maurice's language would not been have readily understood when he stated, "The one thought that possesses
me the most is this, that we have been dosing our
people with religion, when what they want is not this
but the living God."[9] That kind of language was not
much understood then, but came to be more familiar
in the era when Karl Barth, Reinhold Niebuhr, and
others were teaching. Maurice, like Kierkegaard, contrasted God and religion, God and pietism.

The second theme I want to focus on is Maurice's
idea of "eternal life." In 1853, he was expelled from
his professorship on the faculty of King's College, London, an Anglican theological school, for having unsound views and teachings about the doctrine of
eternal punishment. The orthodoxy of the day was
that those who are saved are rewarded in everlasting

happiness, and those who are lost are rewarded in everlasting punishment. Time was thought to be the common medium for both the lost and the saved. Maurice rebelled against that notion; he said "eternal" did not mean "time," but is in fact to be contrasted with time. "Eternal" means another dimension. God is eternal, and to have eternity is to have a life that is shared with God, which is the state of the saved. Those who lose out—and Maurice was very clear that we need to warn ourselves that we might lose out—cannot have anything eternal. They have cut themselves off from God and are missing eternity. The contrast is thus between those who have eternal life, the life with God, and those who may lose eternal life, life with God.

Maurice arrived at this idea by applying the word *aionios* ("eternal") in a way that he believed was strictly biblical (and was certainly strictly Platonist, because a lot of Platonism was in his thought). And he refused to apply the category of everlastingness either to salvation or to loss, though loss was indeed a grave possibility. Well, just as the language of everlastingness meant nothing to him, with that particular Johannine kind of doctrine on which he laid hold, it is equally fair to say that his language meant very little to his contemporaries. Subsequent Anglican theology—and theology in general—has come, I think, to appreciate what Maurice was getting at. His liberation from King's College, London set him free for a very large ministry as a pastor and preacher, and it enabled him to reach many more people who had been left untouched by the more conventional theologians of the time.[10]

The third theme in Maurice's life, and one that had far-reaching significance, is Christian Socialism. Maurice called himself a Christian Socialist and he belonged to a group that included Charles Kingsley,

J.M.F. Ludlow, and others. But what did the term "socialism" mean? It certainly did not mean Marxism. Nor did it mean the political doctrine of socialism as it came to be defined: the nationalization of the means of production, distribution, and exchange, so that you have a state economy replacing an economy of private capitalism. No, Maurice was thinking not in ideological terms, but in practical terms about what was happening in the country. It was the time of a great upsurge—a cry of liberation for the oppressed industrial community. It was the era of the Chartists, a somewhat undefined revolutionary movement in the community among those who who had suffered so much from the Industrial Revolution.

Even though he had no particular ideology about it, Maurice was sure that the church must be there as part of this upsurge alongside those who were in need of liberation. By Christian Socialism, he meant no more than Christians identifying themselves with aspirations for justice and a better way of life. He made it clear these were Christian themes—and could be even further Christianized if they were insufficiently Christian to start with! This is how Maurice described his aim: "Christian Socialism is the only title which will define our object, and will commit us at once to the conflict we must engage in sooner or later with the *Unsocial Christians* and the *Unchristian Socialists*."[11]

Maurice and his colleagues undertook a number of practical steps. They participated in the shaping of some initial trade unions (though such organizations were not called that at the time). They also assisted in the founding and development of cooperative societies, a new thing at the time, and Maurice himself founded an institution called the "Working Men's College," which spread higher education among all sorts of people who were outside the university and college orbits. (Incidentally, this college still exists today.)

Finally it must be noted that the theme of Christian Socialism was to Maurice an intensely theological one. Maurice had come to find that the Trinity was a doctrine he cared passionately about, and so we find Maurice saying in a letter to Kingsley:

> The Name into which we were baptized, the Name which was to bind together all nations, comes out to me more and more as that which must at last break these fetters. I can find none of my liberal friends to whom that language does not sound utterly wild and incomprehensible, while the orthodox would give me for the eternal Name the dry dogma of the Trinity—an opinion which I may brag of as *mine*, given me by I know not what councils of noisy doctors and to be retained in spite of the reason, which it is said to contradict—lest I should be cast into hell for rejecting it. I am sure this Name is the infinite all-embracing charity which I may proclaim to publicans and harlots as that in which they are living and moving and having their being, in which they may be raised to the freedom and righteousness and fellowship for which they were created.[12]

Since the Triune God is the creator of the human race, the likeness of His eternal charity dwells in the human race. The Trinity in Unity is the source of human fellowship in those who repent of their self-centered isolation and discover the true principle of their being.[13] Thus Christian Socialism was to Maurice a passionate expression of the faith of the Trinity about which he cared so much.

Now these themes—the church as a divine family, presented on a rather different wavelength from his contemporaries; eternal life, as distinct from everlasting life and everlasting punishment; and Christian Socialism—all came to have immense influence on the churches of England and America. They affected the way people talked about the doctrine of the Church and how they regarded eschatology. I think what is now called Christian social activism was in its earlier phase greatly inspired by Maurice's teachings.

The strange thing is this: at the time he was writing, the scientific revolution was happening all around him, and yet for all his novelty and creativity Maurice was still really pre-scientific in his theological thinking. Biblical criticism had hardly come his way; he did not discuss it and in fact treated the Bible in a very old-fashioned way. He did not seem interested in some of those themes with which liberal theology was eventually going to concern itself. Rather, these theological insights of Maurice's derive from a very simple root of faith in Christ, and Christ as the revelation of God, and Christ as the center of the human race. But one may fairly say that while Maurice's treatment of the Bible was pre-scientific and pre-critical, his approach would leave one unintimidated by the Higher Criticism. And in fact Maurice's influence made it possible for people subsequently to learn from this academic study of the Bible without being alarmed, frightened, or thrown in over their heads.

The scientific revolution of the nineteenth century was influencing theology then in two particular respects. First of all, if God had created the world through an evolutionary process, then that brought a new vision of the Creator at work in all creation—the divine imminence in the processes of nature. The upshot was that theology, while being still a theology of redemption and revelation, was to become more than ever a theology concerned about God's activity in the created world.

The second major impact the scientific revolution had on theology was, of course, the rise of scientific-historical studies that brought with them far more historical seriousness than there had been in the past. So we see that theological schools in England and in America were coming to be largely concerned with historical questions. Questions were raised about what happened. What happened in the long, drawn-out process of God's preparation of Israel? What happened in Jesus' time, and in the apostolic age? It was this historical interest that came to dominate for a time. At Oxford, Old Testament studies were most prominent under the leadership of S.R. Driver, while at Cambridge New Testament studies flourished under the leadership of Lightfoot, Westcott, and Hort. [14] Lightfoot and Westcott subsequently became bishops of Durham. The work of these Cambridge scholars was to bring an intense historical seriousness into Christianity itself and into all Christian studies in England and America.

I shall conclude by quoting a remark by one of those Cambridge scholars, F.J.A. Hort. Hort wrote less than the others, although he shared with Westcott in the editing of what is called the "Westcott and Hort Greek Testament." He had taught both botany and theology in the University at an earlier stage as well as theology—I imagine with great competence, or they would not have employed him!—and he was very sensitive to this interplay between revealed theology and the scientific spirit. He discussed these issues in a very striking book of lectures called *The Way, the Truth, the Life*, a book that is basically an unfolding of that sentence in the Fourth Gospel, and he brought that theme to bear on a wide range of human studies. In the course of his lectures, Hort sums up a good deal of his thought in this sentence: "Truth of revelation remains inert till it has been appropriated by a human working of recognition which is hard to distinguish from that of discovery."[15]

God reveals. Truth comes from Him. It is His truth. And yet our minds and consciences in receiving it are doing something very like discovery. Is that not the spirit of real theology, which the Anglican tradition tries to pursue? And is it not the method that goes back to our Lord's own method of parabolic teaching?

Charles Gore and Liberal Catholicism

WE SAW THAT the Victorian age was for Anglicans a time of conflict and that three different schools of thought were involved in that conflict, namely, the Tractarians, the Evangelicals, and the Liberals. We also saw that F. D. Maurice was a lonely figure, somewhat apart from the theological parties of his time, who said things that were hard to understand at the time, but were seen to be very significant in later periods. Meanwhile, in America two prominent people appeared who are important to mention. The first was Phillips Brooks, who became Bishop of Massachusetts.[1] Phillips Brooks was not a profound theologian, but he was a great Christian preacher who put the Incarnation and the person of Christ at the center of his preaching, and he preached Christ in a way that had something of the spirit of Maurice's words, "Christ is in every man." When I was a seminarian, one of the required books was Phillips Brooks' *Lectures on Preaching*,[2] for which I have been always been grateful.

The other figure was William Porcher DuBose, who, I think, was one of the great figures of the American Episcopal Church and who also resembled Maurice in being a rather isolated, prophetic theologican.[3] DuBose was born in 1836 and had a curious history. He was a soldier in the Confederate army in the Civil

War, where he spent part of the time as a competent soldier and part of the time as a chaplain. DuBose was severely wounded in the war—to the point of being thought dead. After the war he emerged as a scholar and a theologian on the faculty of the University of the South, which came to life again after the Civil War. And there DuBose held a chair until 1908.

He wrote some books that are hard to describe because they do not fit into ordinary categories. The best known is *The Gospel in the Gospels*, which sets forth DuBose's constant theme that in the Incarnation, God manifests what it means for God to be God. In his suffering and death Christ manifests what it means to be Christ and, furthermore, in Christ humanity realizes what it means to be human. Let me give you two quotations from this book.

> We speak of the incredible and impossible self-lowering or self-emptying of God in becoming man or in undergoing the death of the cross. Is the act in which love becomes perfect a contradiction or a compromise of the divine nature? Is God not God or least God in the moment in which He is most loved? Where before Christ, or otherwise than in Christ, in whom He humbled Himself to become man, and then humbled Himself with and in man to suffer what man must needs suffer in order to become what God would fain make him—and the highest and best that even God can make him—I say where before Christ, or where now otherwise than in Christ and in the cross of the divine suffering together with and for man, where in all the story of the universe is love so love, or God so God![4]

What it means to be God is seen in the Incarnation, which is not a contradiction of deity. As with God, so with man. I give another quotation:

I would describe Christianity in its largest sense to
be the fulfillment of God in the world through the
fulfillment of the world in God. This assumes that
the world is completed in man, in whom also God is
completed in the world. And so, God, the world, and
man are at once completed in Jesus Christ—who, as
He was the *logos* or thought of all in the divine fore-
knowledge of the part, so also is He the *telos* or end
of all in the predestination of the future.[5]

Well, when I was a very young seminarian, I was
grateful that DuBose was on the reading list.

Now, apart form the inevitable partialities and mis-
understandings, what was the serious area of intellectual conflict in the Victorian period? I think for
Christians it was the problem of holding together the
"givenness" of God's revelation in Christ and salvation
through the Christian history, on the one hand, and
on the other hand the exploration of the meaning of
the world through the rapidly growing sciences.

Before the nineteenth century ended, there came
about something of a synthesis, which took shape in
the volume *Lux Mundi: A Series of Studies in the Religion of the Incarnation*, edited by Charles Gore, then
a fairly young Oxford scholar, and his colleagues.[6] *Lux
Mundi* is described as an attempt to put the Catholic
faith in its right relationship to modern intellectual
and moral problems. That attempt was criticized, because others thought it would be better to put modern
intellectual and moral problems into relationship to
the Catholic faith. In fact, you cannot do one without
doing the other. In what I am going to say, I have in
mind not only this volume of essays, *Lux Mundi*, published in 1889, and Charles Gore's book, *The Incarnation of the Son of God*, published in 1891, but also a
whole range of Anglican writings that came out
during the next thirty years or more, and that very

much embodied the same enterprise, method, and spirit.[7]

What were some of the bases for this synthesis? Let me sum it up by first saying, "Creation." I quote the essay "The Christian Doctrine of God" by Aubrey Moore in *Lux Mundi*:

> The one absolutely impossible conception of God, in the present day, is that which represents Him as an occasional Visitor. Science had pushed the deist God farther and farther away, and at the moment when it seemed as if He would be thrust out altogether, Darwinism appeared, and under the disguise of a foe, did the work of a friend. It has conferred upon philosophy and religion an inestimable benefit, by showing us that we must choose between two alternatives. Either God is everywhere present in nature, or He is nowhere. He cannot be here and not there.[8]

That language, although it seemed strange to some, came to be a presupposition of this Anglican synthesis.

A second major line of thinking involved in the synthesis was the Incarnation.[9] In the context of the doctrine of creation, Christ is presented as both natural and supernatural. Natural, yes—Christ is part of and the climax of a divine process in history. As organic nature fulfills the potentialities of inorganic nature, and humanity fulfills the potentialities of organic nature, so Jesus, when he appears in history, fulfills the potentiality of the whole series: subhumanity, humanity, the New Humanity. You see, it is one of a series. And so Charles Gore dared to say that the Incarnation of Christ is something natural, but at the same time supernatural.

Now what about this later category? By "supernatural," Gore means that the Incarnation represents a new order that cannot be understood in terms of lesser categories. He also intends supernatural to be understood in this sense: the divine process has been wrecked and ravaged by sin, so God's problem is not just the completion of a series, but also the restoration of humanity and the world. It is this strongly evangelical note that breaks into the affirmation that Jesus and the Incarnation are both supernatural and natural. Because of the emphasis on the supernatural, Charles Gore and the Anglicanism of his time and afterward did not hesitate to say that the miraculous is an inevitable, integral part of the Incarnation.

Let me hasten to add that they did not say that miracles proved the deity of Jesus, like so many portents; rather, they thought that the Incarnation was a supernatural intervention. Therefore, miraculous happenings are totally congruous with the fact of the Incarnation. Furthermore, for Gore and his colleagues, miracles were significant because they emphasized the divine freedom in the process of God's putting the world right. Human beings have misused freedom in disrupting the created world in disastrous ways. Miracles are the way God uses His freedom, which is not subject to known physical laws, in the process of putting to rights a world that has gone radically astray. Even so, these theologians sometimes said that the miraculous is natural as well as supernatural, because it is a part of this new order in the divine series. Gore and the others frequently quoted the famous dictum of St. Augustine, "A miracle is not what is contrary to nature, but that which is contrary to nature as it is known. A miracle is new to what we have known and experienced so far, but perhaps it is not new to some higher purpose of God, which for all we know may be just as rational as any of our ideas.

The third basis of this Anglican synthesis, then, after the doctrines of Creation and Incarnation, was inspiration.[10] Inspiration figures very prominently, and one of the essays in *Lux Mundi* was called "The Holy Spirit and Inspiration," written by Gore himself. It has a wonderfully comprehensive pattern. The Holy Spirit is at work in all creation. The Holy Spirit is at work in a special and unique way in the Scriptures, not inspiring texts so much as inspiring those who wrote the texts. Indeed the Holy Spirit inspires Israel, the People of God, in all the ups and downs of its history, in writings of very different kinds, to be the very witness to God. It led on to the outburst of the Holy Spirit in the apostolic age, which inspired the apostolic authors to write about Jesus in diverse ways.

It was at this point that a controversy arose. Following the arguments of literary and historical criticism, the standard interpretation was that we need not regard the Book of Jonah, for example, as necessarily historical. The story of three days and three nights in the belly of the whale—might that not be allegory? parable? symbol? Similarly, we need not ascribe all the psalms to David. Critical study places the psalms in many different periods; some are set in the time of David, while others were written at different stages of history. (I had an Old Testament professor named R. H. Kennet who insisted on putting all the psalms in the Maccabean period. This became such an obsession for him that the poor man was known for having a "maccabee" in his bonnet!) The crisis was this: the gospels report Jesus as saying that Jonah was in the whale's belly. So does not the authority of Jesus authenticate the old-fashioned point of view? Again, when Jesus argues with the scribes about laboring on the Sabbath, he seems to refer to David as the author of Psalm 110. Does not that settle it? Thus there was a conflict between this new interpretation of Scripture and what was seen as Jesus' authority in authenticating a literalist point of view.

Charles Gore answered these critics by saying that the human mind of Jesus was limited to the knowledge of his day. While He had the mind of God in perfectly revealing God's character and purpose, he was not there to anticipate all knowledge, all sciences, all human investigations. In fact, in such matters Jesus was not setting out to teach humanity, for He had only the knowledge of his time. This meant, in a rather incidental way, that the great question of *kenosis* also came to a head.

Now what did Gore mean by *kenosis*? He and his colleagues taught that in the Incarnation, there was a "self-limitation" of the divine wisdom of Jesus. While Jesus was an infallible revelation of God, he had a mind that was subject to the genuine conditions of his time. That is, of course, a very important matter, one reaching far beyond biblical criticism into areas of history and metaphysics, and so on. But it is fair to say that in that era, the idea of *kenosis*, of the self-limitation or self-emptying of the divine mind in the Incarnation, came to be common ground among nearly all Anglican exponents, from *Lux Mundi* in 1889, right through to O.C. Quick's work in systematic theology, *Doctrines of the Creed*, in 1939, and even beyond.

This concept of *kenosis* was expressed in a wide variety of ways. On the Continent, in some Lutheran circles, some very radical ideas of *kenosis* had appeared, suggesting that the Son of God abandoned certain divine attributes in the Incarnation, such as omnipotence, although he still retained the attribute of love. That was felt to be a meaningless mythology, however, because Christianity teaches that God's omnipotence and love are intermingled one with the other. How can you abandon one attribute and retain the other? Those rather mythological concepts of *kenosis* never, I think, gained much ground in England. Gore himself used rather ambiguous language. He wrote in a footnote to his original text that Jesus "'beggared Himself' of Divine prerogatives to put Himself in our place." In the next edition Gore modified that to "He 'beggared Himself' of the exercise of Divine prerogatives..."[11] thereby revealing that on the metaphysics of the matter there was, as there must be, a good deal of obscurity.

The main point is this: the Anglican teachers of that period did not hesitate to combine a belief in the divine Christ with a belief in Christ's total participation in the conditions of human life. They would say that if that belief is paradoxical, the paradox needs to be located in the region of the divine power and love. (Perhaps that passage form DuBose I quoted at the beginning may illuminate the matter a little. It certainly illuminated the matter for me a good deal when I first read it.) Of course, behind all thoughts about the Incarnation there lies that great sentence of St. Augustine, "So deeply had human pride sunk us, that nothing but Divine Humility could raise us." Theories of *kenosis* for all their clumsiness, are attempts to take that divine humility with real seriousness.[12]

This teaching of the *Lux Mundi* school, which emphasized creation, incarnation, and inspiration, could claim a great symmetry and coherence. It synthesized historic faith and contemporary knowledge, as well as presenting a coherent shape and pattern of Christian teaching and doctrine.

Consider the following. God creates the world by a process of creation that is compatible with the findings of Darwin. The human being is the climax of the process. Then there comes the Fall—not to be identified with what happened in the Garden of Eden, but with a deep estrangement of the human race from the true path of godliness. While human progress—that is, moral, spiritual, and intellectual progress—is a great reality, there is also a tragic deviation.

Humankind cannot be rescued into its right shape apart from an act of God coming to the rescue. God prepares the way with the action of the *logos* in many cultures and religions, and particularly in Israel, through the Incarnation, He gives Himself to humanity. The Incarnation, with both cross and resurrection as its climax, is the divine self-giving, enabling men and women through the now-indwelling Spirit to give themselves back to God in lives that are really a re-creation of human nature in Christ. Finally, the Holy Spirit working through the church, in word and sacrament, is the continuance in every age of this work of reconciliation and new creation.

The coherence of Christian doctrine presented in an Anglican way has two aspects that we must look at further. The first is the concept of the development of doctrine, and the second is a strong emphasis on history.

Let us think first of the development of doctrine. Recall how John Henry Newman justified his embracing Rome as his new church on the basis of his concept of development. There have been different ideas of development, however, and we need to distinguish between them. One idea of development claims that, although certain truths were possessed by the early church, they were not yet visibly manifest for people to see. Thus a kind of doctrinal development found among Roman Catholics holds that the doctrine of the Immaculate Conception always existed, but no one told us about it until 1854. This view, then, states that certain things were always there, in the bag, but the contents were let out at different periods of history, progressively, according to the capacity of Christians to receive them.

The other way of thinking about development is that doctrine must be open, accessible to the faithful at every stage of history. Under the guidance of the

Holy Spirit, we are given fresh understandings and fresh articulation of what has been revealed originally in all kinds of hidden seeds. If in the apostolic age, for instance, Jesus was already being worshipped as divine (the fourth evangelist describes St. Thomas as saying, "My Lord and my God"), then what happened several centuries later at the Council of Nicea was the outcome—the development, the intellectual expression—of something that was already present at a much earlier stage.

Or take the doctrine of the Holy Trinity. It is very clear that a triune experience of God exists from the early days of Christianity. There is the God to whom they pray as *Abba*, Father; there is God in Jesus, whom they find themselves worshipping as divine; and there is God the Holy Spirit within them, enabling their response. And yet they are sure there is but one God. What later happens in the creeds, and in the teachings of St. Augustine or the Cappodocian Fathers, is the expansion of a belief that was there from the beginning. Characteristic of the Anglican view is this: it allows for development in doctrine because it does not hold a "fundamentalist" position. Yet at the same time, development is always checked by the classic Anglican appeal to history and to reason. Is this developed formulation, then, a reasonable understanding and manifestation of something for which there really is evidence from antiquity?

The other characteristic of this kind of Anglicanism was and still is a strong emphasis upon history itself. To Bishop Gore, the historicity of Jesus and the apostolic age was very secure indeed. Theologians used the same critical methods that had been used with the Old Testament, but they were confident that in the gospels—despite certain elaborations and interpretations—we do have authentic history. The Anglican appeal to history was made to carry a very great weight.

These historical events were the basis for the Christian faith in God, of the Christian understanding of God. But it could not handle all that weight; while we can appeal to history, we need to supplement that by an appeal to experience as well.

That became an area of controversy, too. For several decades of Anglican life, this controversy tended to concentrate on miracles, particularly the miracle of the virgin birth of Jesus and the miracle of Jesus' bodily resurrection. Bishop Gore and his colleagues, while claiming to be liberal—and indeed they were— were certain that the historical evidence for these things was very sound. It was only a kind of negative, liberal protestant prejudice that would cause people to deny these miracles that are affirmed in the Creed.

Consequently, there came about a notorious controversy between Bishop Gore, who at the time was Bishop of Oxford, and Dr. Herbert Hensley Henson, who subsequently became Bishop of Hereford, about this very point.[13] In order for us to understand this controversy, we have to distinguish two totally different phenomena in understanding and belief and approach.

Think of Mr. A and Mr. B. Mr. A says, "Of course I believe Jesus to be a man—a great prophet, but a man. Nothing supernatural about it, nothing miraculous about it. And the best I might accept in terms of Christology might be a kind of adoptionism, so the virgin birth and the bodily resurrection are not only incredible by my standards, they are also pretty irrelevant." That is one position. But now think of our hypothetical Mr. B, who says this: "I believe in a divine Christ, a Savior who is indeed supernatural. And I am ready to believe that miraculous events happened in connection with the coming and the life of Christ. But looking at it honestly and cautiously, I cannot be quite sure what really happened in connection with his birth, because the narratives might be of a symbolic kind; and I cannot be quite sure what happened on Easter Day. For though I am quite sure that Jesus was and is alive, and though I am sure that something stupendous happened, I cannot with my historical conscience be really sure exactly what."

Now it seems to me very important indeed to distinguish the position of Mr. A and Mr. B. If I may enlarge a bit on the position of Mr. B, I would say this: I am not a Mr. B myself, because as you would expect of an old man, I am pretty conservative about most things. But it is very, very important to understand these issues. For myself, believing Jesus to be the divine Savior and God incarnate, I would say it is not the least surprising that miraculous things really happened. Equally, it would not be the least surprising if the gospel narratives were of a symbolic, poetic kind witnessing a symbolic and poetic way to the Christian experience of a divine Savior.

I think the Charles Gore kind of Liberal Catholicism did not reckon with this area of thought as fully and fairly as it might have. Christianity is an historical faith, which believes that God manifests Himself through certain events and saves the world through certain events. Drop that and you have made Christianity a different thing altogether. But our knowledge of God must always consist of both an appeal to historical fact, of which there is plenty, and an appeal to experience—the experience of the first Christians and our experience as well.

At a later phase, a form of Liberal Catholicism arose that still clung to history, but also put a good deal more emphasis on the complementary appeal to experience. If you read the book of essays called *Essays Catholic and Critical* (1926), you will find it to be in the *Lux Mundi* tradition, while also including more about the appeal to experience.

I would like to end by suggesting that holding the appeal to history and to experience in balance is really the key both to New Testament studies and to theology as a whole. In theology, where the history of God in Christ is so central, we must appeal to experience in order to be credible: the experience of the first Christians, of Christians down through the ages, and of ourselves. And in the area of New Testament studies, we are trying to find out what really happened. What was said and done by the Sea of Galilee? What was said and done in the streets of Jerusalem, and on the hill of Calvary? But we are also concerned in New Testament studies with the experience of those first witnesses to Christ the Savior that caused them to write at all—the tremendous experience that left them and us exclaiming, "My Lord and my God!"

William Temple

WE NOW COME in the course of our lectures to one of the greatest of Anglicans in this or any other century, William Temple. Temple was the son of a previous Archbishop of Canterbury, Frederick Temple,[1] and, interestingly enough, had the approach to theology of an amateur. He did not pursue either biblical or patristic studies very rigorously, for his major intellectual interests lay outside the specific fields in which theologians for the most part worked. Temple's mind was trained in philosophy, Plato among the ancients and Hegel among more modern philosophers. He had a wide interest in the arts, the sciences, social problems, politics, history—human interests and human concerns of every kind. And yet although somewhat of an amateur in theological studies, Temple was, perhaps as much as anyone who has ever lived, a theologian. The whole of his wide interests, intellectual and personal, were concerned with a relationship to God, and it was his way to ask constantly, how does God bear upon this? How does this bear upon our understanding of God? Indeed, in this connection, Temple used to insist again and again that "religious experience" does not mean a particular region of experience that only concerns piety, religious exercises, and a conscious religious practice. No, he insisted that religious experience is for the believing person the whole of experience, of everything and everybody seen in relationship to God. The appeal, then, to religious experience meant for Temple the total human experience seen in some kind of relationship to God.

William Temple had an immense range of interests in the life of the community: educational and scientific, political and social. While he gave an immense impetus to what is called "Christian social action," at the same time he emphasized the priority of worship for the Christian life. Temple's teaching about the priority of worship sounded strange in the context in which it was preached, where it was readily believed that the important thing for Christianity was social action—serving your neighbor and finding God in the service of your neighbor. If going to church and worshipping God helped in these processes, then so much the better. It was that rather superficial view of the relationship between worship and Christian living that Temple again and again radically challenged. "It is often said," Temple wrote, "that conduct is supremely important and worship helps it. The truth is that worship is supremely important and conduct tests it."[2] Men and women exist to glorify their Creator. That is the true end of our being. We are created in order to be worshippers, and that is the true description of life here and of life eternally. However, because God is loving and righteous, there is no genuine worship of God that is not reflected in the urgent, practical, outgoing service of humanity. But this urgent, practical, outgoing service of humanity, because it has God as its author, brings us back again to the praise and glory of God from whom all good things come. That is Temple's teaching about the imperative character of Christian social activity and witness.

Perhaps one of the remarkable things about Temple's influence was the way he devoted his life to so many causes and interests far beyond the frontiers of theology and the church. While participating in these activities wholeheartedly, he was also quietly and vocally bearing witness to the primacy of the glory of God for the understanding of human life.

With these wide interests, which had the Bible and the Christian revelation as their center, Temple always sought unity and synthesis. He held the Church of England together during the war, from 1942 to 1944, a very difficult time indeed, mainly through his conviction that beneath every erroneous position there lies some truth. And when confronted with positions that were palpably erroneous and silly, his line was not to expose and denounce, but rather to say, "Come here, let us look at it. This is what you believe." And he could draw out from that view something—even some little piece—that really was true and therefore to be revered. Consequently Temple could engage in a dialogue with the other person, and show how this small fragment of truth was but a fragment, and would have its best chance if it would be synthesized with other aspects of the truth. This was and is a marvelous gift to have.

It was this synthetic gift that made Temple a unifier in a rather contentious Church of England, and a force for unity in the early days of the ecumenical movement. He aspired to be a unifier to an extent that some thought was rather paradoxical. I remember an occasion when I was invited as a very young man to listen in on a conference for some high-powered theological giants. There was Temple himself, along with some ardent Anglo-Catholic, as well as Reinhold Niebuhr, Emil Brunner, and a very conservative Lutheran of what you might call the Missouri Synod stamp. The evening was spent in an intense debate over an apparently irreconcilable opposites, and I recall Temple saying as he retired to his room, "Well, we have got a lot to synthesize!" 3 And sure enough, he spent a half hour constructing a synthesis that he then produced at breakfast the next morning.

It was this great belief in his own powers of synthesis that provoked W. R. Matthew to say that, if Temple had been present at the Council of Nicea, there would have been a synthesis between the Orthodox and the Arians! Now I am caricaturing Temple just a little, but his belief in his own considerable ability to synthesize was extremely valuable to Christianity at the time.

In terms of theology and philosophy, it was Temple's conviction that the idealistic philosophy so prevalent at the time, a kind of Oxbridge version of Hegelianism, covered a large ground of human belief and activity. Furthermore, he thought, it was important to show not just that human beings were spiritual, and that spirituality was diffused in the world, but that this spirituality had its illuminating focus and center in Jesus of Nazareth, believed in as God incarnate. That is to say, Temple's quest was a kind of Christian metaphysics embracing all knowledge and all human activity, with the Incarnation at the center. Of course, the attempt to establish such a belief presupposes a philosophical climate that is a great deal more friendly to religion and religious experience than is often the case.

Temple's largest book, *Nature, Man and God*, is the fullest exposition of his thought, but I think two books that are easier to grasp and more likely to be lasting are *Christus Veritas*, and *Readings in St. John's Gospel*. The former is a book about the Incarnation as the key to the climax of the creative process, while the latter is a series of meditations on the Fourth Gospel from a somewhat conservative point of view, a deep meditation on the Fourth Gospel's statement, "He that hath seen me hath seen the Father."[4]

Indeed, Temple was wont to say that his whole theological effort was to draw out the implications of just that sentence. He explored it in two ways that were very striking and made a special impact upon the thought of those who learned from him. First, he saw the Johannine conception of the divine glory revealed in the Passion as the key to our understanding of divine sovereignty. God's eternal sovereignty is the sovereignty of sacrificial love embodied in the Passion story. He thus helped those who were perplexed about seeing the deity of Christ and the sovereignty of God together with the very human limitations of Jesus. It is just in the midst of these limitations, Temple said, that the power, glory, and majesty of God is most manifest.

Let me offer you a striking instance of the length to which Temple carried this thought. He was, of course, devoted to the Gospel of St. John, particularly to the story of the Passion and the Resurrection. Here in the self-giving love of the Crucified is the key to God's eternal glory. Temple brought together the cry of dereliction in St. Mark's gospel with the divine glory, and commented on the cry of dereliction, *"Eloi, Eloi, lama sabachtani?"* He asked how that could be compatible with Jesus' divinity, and wrote in reply: "God is never more God than when in bearing the load of the world's suffering, he feels Himself to be deserted by God." (That is the sort of language with which Moltmann has made us more familiar lately.[5]) It may be stated in a way that is overly rhetorical and paradoxical, but we can see his deep conviction that the God who underwent the humiliation and suffering is indeed the God who is glorious and sovereign.

A second aspect of his cross-centered understanding of divine power and glory was Temple's very characteristic treatment of God's suffering. Traditional theologians still went on emphasizing the impassibility of

God in the manner of the teaching of the church fathers, but Temple himself sharply challenged this idea that God is not capable of suffering. I quote his words, "All that we can suffer...is within the Divine experience; He has known it all Himself."[6] God is never passive; nothing happens to Him without His consent. But the traditional term "impassibility" really meant "incapable of suffering", and this, Temple says, is "almost wholly false." Almost! In that word there was a slight drawing back. Temple seems to explain the "almost" by his sentence, "It is truer to say that there is suffering in God than that God suffers."[7] And why? "[The suffering] is an element in the joy of the triumphant sacrifice."[8] God suffers through identifying Himself and sharing and bearing all the sufferings of His creatures. Yet He does not suffer as one who is defeated or frustrated, because God's suffering is part of that love which has already triumphed.

Now we come to another characteristic teaching of William Temple, namely, his teaching on revelation. He insisted that God does not—indeed, cannot—reveal Himself in particular events or in a particular person, Jesus, unless He is also revealing Himself far and wide, within the totality of human experience. Unless we know something of God here, there, and everywhere, we are not going to know Him when He manifests Himself in a particular way in and through Jesus. Temple emphasized the potentially revelatory character of all experience as a kind of background to the specific revelation of God in Christ. Moreover, when it comes to the specific revelation of God in Christ, God is revealing Himself in that particular way because God is personal, and He can make Himself fully known to humanity only through a person in relationship to other persons. Thus the personal revelation of God in Christ is what validates all the rest of revelation. What God reveals in Christ is Himself, the Lord of all that diffused revelation.[9]

But how does God reveal Himself through Jesus? Temple insisted that revelation cannot be through propositions; it takes place instead through an event and through mind. God does certain things, certain things happen in the person of Jesus, and human minds are inspired to interpret what happens in words. Persons, events, and minds are the media of revelations, but propositions alone cannot be the medium.[10]

This concept of revelation as personal or relational, not propositional, had immense influence and popularity. God does not tell us things we are to memorize. God shows Himself to us in a person, and by knowing that person we know God.

People inevitably said, however, that if inspired propositions like the creeds have a necessary place in this understanding of revelation, does it not mean that they also have a place in the process of revelation itself? Temple would be the first to acknowledge that scriptural statements, the creeds, and the pronouncements of the Church Fathers all have their necessary place within the understanding of the process of revelation. But this statement showed up Temple's oversimplification of his theory of revelation.

If we think of it in the simplest terms, God is revealed in a person and that leads to the response that Jesus is Lord. That is knowledge of a person as well as a proposition about the revelation. Any doctrinal view of Jesus is in fact both personal and a response to that revelation in the form of a proposition. The latter response should not be rejected as "propositional," for any revelation includes not only the personal element, but also the language of imagery and proposition used to interpret the event.

With regard to Temple's Christian social witness certainly had immense influence, and I wonder if there has ever been a Christian teacher who witnessed so widely to his conviction about Jesus Christ in so many areas of the life of the community. He spoke out against capitalism as it was developing, and argued that in principle a socialist state could be nearer to the mind of Christ than a capitalist state.[11] (That point of view, of course, was at the time very unpopular indeed.) Some other unpopular stands of Temple's included speaking against the war guilt clauses in the Treaty of Versailles while addressing the Disarmament Conference in Geneva. Temple agreed that the Germans were guilty of the aggressive policy that caused the war, but to place all the blame on Germany ignored the selfish and belligerent background of international relations in Europe.[12] Linked with this witness was Temple's protest against the bombing of cities and heavily populated areas by England and her allies in World War Two. He pleaded that the bombing should be of military targets, not obliteration bombing designed to destroy whole cities and their civilian inhabitants.[13]

Temple was also among the first of the Christian leaders to speak out against the death penalty, arguing that murder is the crime of treating human life as if it were not sacred. To punish the murderer by killing him is to take one further step in the devaluation of human life and is, therefore, immoral. Temple's line on that was, in the Thirties, rather unpopular and solitary, but when the death penalty was abolished in England in the Sixties, church leaders had rather belatedly begun to take the same line themselves. In that way Temple was courageously prophetic.[14]

In the sphere of economics, Temple again held views that were unpopular. He invoked Thomas Aquinas' concept of the just price in his continual criticism of the banking system. Temple alleged that the system of banking, by treating money in an arbitrary way, gave it an artificial value that only enriched particular people rather than letting money serve its simple purpose as a medium of exchange. Of course the bankers did not want Thomas Aquinas quoted to them, nor did they understand the relevance of his thought! (I think that Temple was indeed talking a kind of good sense that still needs to be affirmed.)

Now I have not given an adequate account of Temple's theology, which because of its comprehensiveness is a task perhaps beyond anyone. I have spoken of his main theological themes and some of the ways in which those themes were brought to bear upon the life of the community. Temple was seeking synthesis: synthesis between conflicting elements within his own church, synthesis within Christendom through his pioneering efforts in the ecumenical movement, and synthesis between the Christian Gospel and the many forms of human knowledge and activity. As I mentioned earlier, these efforts presupposed an intellectual climate favorable to Christianity, as well as the existence of moral values in the community to which Christianity could appeal. But the world was becoming a much darker place than it was when Temple began his work as a divine and a teacher.

In 1942 William Temple became Archbishop of Canterbury, and in 1944 he died of a heart attack at the age of sixty-three.[15] In his last years Temple said some very striking things about the change in theological perspective. Acknowledging that the world was becoming a very different place, were he starting to do theology again he would have to do it very differently. Temple was wonderfully humble and self-critical, as the following quotations from letters and articles suggest.

As I review in thought the result of our fourteen
years of labor, I am conscious of a certain transition
of interest in our minds, as in the minds of theologians all over the world....A theology of the Incarnation tends to be Christo-centric metaphysic. ...A
theology of Redemption (though, of course, Redemption has its great place in the former) tends rather
to sound the prophetic note; it is more ready to
admit that much in this evil world is irrational and
strictly unintelligible; and it looks to the coming of
the Kingdom as a necessary preliminary to the full
comprehension of much that now is. If the security
of the nineteenth century, already shattered in
Europe, finally crumbles away in our own country,
we shall be pressed more and more towards a theology of Redemption. In this we shall be coming
closer to the New Testament....If we began our
work again today, its perspectives would be different. But it is not our function to pioneer.[16]

Temple is of course speaking of himself and those of
his generation who fashioned an incarnational metaphysic. It was time for a new generation to take up a
new task in a far different world.

Again, in describing the changed situation in theology, Temple had this to say:

When the older theologians offer to men fashioned
by such influences a Christian map of the world,
these rightly refuse to listen. The world of today is
one of which no Christian map is possible. It must
be changed by Christ into something very unlike itself before a Christian map of it is possible. We
used to believe in the sovereignty of the God of love
a great deal too lightheartedly. I have much more
understanding now than I had in 1906 or there-
abouts of Bishop Gore's passionate outburst at a
meeting of the Synthetic Society: "If it were not for
the miracles, and supremely the Resurrection, I
should see no more reason for supposing that God is

revealed in Jesus Christ than that He is revealed in Nero."[17]

Then Temple continued:

There is a new task for theologians today. We cannot come to the men of today saying, "You will find that all your experience fits together in a harmonious system if you will only look at it in the illumination of the Gospel." ...Our task with this world is not to explain it but to convert it. Its need can be met, not by the discovery of its own immanent principle in signal manifestation through Jesus Christ, but only by the shattering impact upon its self-sufficiency and arrogance of the Son of God, crucified, risen and ascended, pouring forth that explosive and disruptive energy which is the Holy Ghost. He is the source of fellowship, and all true fellowship comes from him. But in order to fashion true fellowship in such a world as this, and out of such men and women as we are, He must first break up those fellowships with which we have been deluding ourselves. Christ said that the effect of His coming would be to set much at variance. We must expect the movement of His spirit among us to produce sharper divisions as well as deeper unity.[18]

Those were prophetic words, acknowledging that the world was so dark that only a theology of redemption made sense anymore.

Finally, looking into the future, Temple wrote this:

We must dig the foundations deeper than we did in pre-war years, or in the inter-war years when we developed our post-war thoughts. And we must be content with less imposing structures. One day theology will take up again its larger and serener task, and offer to a new Christendom its Christian map of life, its Christo-centric metaphysics. But that day can barely dawn while any who are now already concerned with theology are still alive.[19]

The death of Temple and the end of the Second World War meant for Anglicanism and for all Christian theology the shock of a transition into a much grimmer world. What theology does, and what Anglican theology can do in this far darker world, we shall be considering in the next chapter.

Recall these two very wonderful men, Charles Gore and William Temple. They were very different. Looking back on them, I remember how when I was a young man Charles Gore was beginning to be seen as too conservative. We looked for something a bit more liberal and contemporary, and found it in William Temple. Looking back to Temple now, whose teaching used to inspire me very greatly, it seems rather dated—it seems to be rather the easy world of the Oxbridge of the Thirties. But Charles Gore, who at the time seemed more old-fashioned and more remote, now seems to be more like the kind of timeless Hebrew prophet who in any age and place can tell us about the righteousness of God. Yet both men were such giants, as Anglicans and theologians and Christians, who helped people to say to themselves, "If a man of that intellectual integrity can accept the Christian faith in God, well, I think I can accept it too." And that is a tremendous thing to say of any man or woman. Of either one of them it can also be said, "Here is a man who by his amazing personal humility brings God real and near to me." Indeed, let all this be summed up in those great old words of St. Irenaeus, "The glory of God is the human being alive. The life of humanity is the vision of God."

Biblical Theology and
Christian Renewal

WORLD WAR TWO ended in 1945, and I think history will recall that the end of the war soon saw some wonderful events in the renewal of Christianity, after the shattering effects of war on nations and churches. I can think of three ways in which this renewal was apparent. Within Germany itself the Christian churches recovered miraculously after the horrors of the Hitler holocaust, and were renewed not only in their own life, but in the spirit of reconciliation with other churches in the world. Just for one example, if you travel to England, do see the rebuilt Coventry Cathedral, and note the signs in various places with their messages of reconciliation and hope between German and English Christians. German money helped rebuild Coventry Cathedral after it was destroyed by bombs during the war.

Amid the exciting recovery of Christianity in the postwar world, what happened to Anglican theology? It had enjoyed a good deal of attention from the world at large and produced some coherence in modern theology under teachers like Temple and his contemporaries. In the postwar world, however, amid a great deal of Christian theological recovery and advancement, Anglican theology became something rather hard to recognize. It seemed to lose coherence and identity, and I believe there were several reasons for this.

One reason lay in the outburst of ecumenical activity. Before the war there had been the "Faith and Order" movement, which drew theologians and churchmen of different traditions together, and the "Life and Work" movement, which brought the Christian social activities of different churches together.[1] These two movements coalesced in the foundation of the World Council of Churches in 1948. In that ecumenical activity, Anglican leaders such as William Temple and Bishop George Bell played a very prominent role. The rise in ecumenism meant that theologians in different churches were now doing together things they had previously done separately. In the excitement generated by all this activity—and it was more than time for that to happen—strong denominational identity no longer seemed to count for much. Furthermore, the particular Anglican triad of Scripture, tradition and reason, far from being an Anglican monopoly, was the very matter that theologians of different traditions were eager to discuss. Thus Anglican identity became less noticeable amid the ecumenical scene in which everybody was being stirred up in a single pot!

A second and less obvious cause of a loss of Anglican identity was the powerful movement known as biblical theology. Biblical theology raised a particular kind of concern about the Bible among both scholars and preachers in the Thirties, Forties, and Fifties. Biblical theology was not fundamentalism—oh no, it employed all the methods of critical study—nor was it a "history of religions" kind of approach, either, because of the depth of its convictions about the Word of God. As hard to define as it was, biblical theology meant an intense preoccupation with the Bible as the center of theology, and, indeed, as the almost exclusive source of theology. The unity of the Bible was emphasized, and the words of the Bible were studied in great depth as containing in themselves divine revelation.

Preaching, therefore, tended toward the exposition of the Bible from within. It was certainly done in a very scholarly fashion, but it overemphasized the unity of the Bible and treated certain questions with a bit more assurance and certainty than a critical mind might have done. In England, teachers like E.C. Hoskyns,[2] C. H. Dodd, and T. W. Manson were prominent in the biblical theology movement, while on the Continent there was the work of Gerhard Kittel. The Kittel lexicon of New Testament Greek acquired a reputation and preeminence no biblical dictionary has ever had before or since. Explore the biblical words in their own way, on their own terms, and you will extract from them a living Gospel.[3]

As a young teacher I was very much involved in this, and for that very reason I find it hard to describe. I must admit I had at the time just a wee bit of skepticism about all the implications. This very assured use of the Bible both by scholars and by preachers was heavily influenced by Karl Barth, a prophetic figure who emphasized the Word of God over against human religion. The influence of Rudolph Bultmann was also important—not that Bultmann's critical theories were ever really accepted, but his reliance on the existential concept of faith was very influential indeed. This movement tended to confine all of theology to the Bible, so whether you were Anglican or Presbyterian or Roman Catholic did not seem to matter.

Still, the biblical theology movement declined, and I think for the following reasons. As I mentioned a moment ago, criticism began to be leveled at the rather simplistic way that the Bible was treated as a unified whole; there is really a great deal more variety of theme in the Bible than they allowed for. Also, while biblical theologians had gotten caught up in certain historical questions about the Bible, they had not resolved any of them. Finally, and most importantly, biblical theology operated too much in a vacuum and did not face the kinds of questions raised by philosophical theologians, particularly with regard to the contemporary world. Although their work could have the power to convert, biblical theologicans found themselves with very little to say in relation to the questions of the contemporary world that needed exploration and answers, despite Karl Barth's recommendation that preachers needed to preach the Gospel with the Bible in one hand and the newspaper in the other.

A third reason for the decline in Anglican identity was this. The postwar theological world had been a very stirring time during which God had raised up a number of great teachers who cut across all denominational lines: Rudolph Bultmann, Karl Barth, Paul Tillich, Dietrich Bonhoeffer in Europe, Thomas Merton in America, and the spiritual teachers of the Eastern Orthodox Church. The very existence of a number of great thinkers, teachers, and prophets who commanded respect regardless of what church they belonged to loosened the hold of denominational identity.

Now, I name these areas—ecumenism, biblical theology, and the great Christian teachers—as reasons why Anglican identity (to name but one denomination) declined. But as time passes, and as the movement of Christian unity grows, people seek also a pattern and shape for Christian unity. If you are really longing for shape in Christian life, and cannot swallow either the papacy or the Missouri Synod, *where do you go?* It was precisely that sort of consideration which made one aware that while we were conscious of losing our Anglican identity, there were lots of other people who greatly revered Anglican identity and wished there was rather more of it. They began to wish that Anglicans would recover the strengths of their own tradition, and began to say to us, "Yes, we do wish you Anglicans would go on being Anglicans. Because if you are preaching that 'God is dead,' that is not the Anglicanism we recognize! Or if you simply preach the latest political or social fad, that is not the Anglicanism we recognize, either."

The reason for other Christians' valuing of Anglican tradition in these years of turmoil was twofold. The first has to do with the relationship between the shape of theology, the Christian life, and the spiritual life. Anglicanism holds together tradition and exploration, especially in the context of worship and liturgy. I think it is that ability which made people very often hunger for what the Anglican Church can give. Of course holding these things together is nothing unique, but doing so through the medium of a given tradition of worship that binds them—that is the Anglican theme. I mentioned earlier that some Continental scholars used to laugh at us for doing our theology to the sound of church bells. I think in the latter years they have been rather envious of us for doing just that!

The second way in which Anglicanism came to be revalued is in relationship to Christian unity. Nobody wants a central church bureaucracy, but Christian unity must have a kind of shape. Believers from other traditions see in the Anglican way something of the shape of the Scriptures, the traditions, the creeds, the sacraments, the apostolic ministry, and the way they are interwoven. Thus whenever there have been actual unions of churches, the Anglican shape has had very great influence indeed. So whenever we tell ourselves that we want, in a sense, to "disappear," there are many who tell us the contrary.

Anglican tradition has in these last years experienced divisive tensions along with the rest of Christendom. And yet I believe there are in Anglicanism God-given strengths for dealing with those tensions. For example, the Sixties witnessed the growth of secularized Christianity and the "death of God" movement, fads needlessly and terribly unsettling to a good many Christians. Still, as William Temple would have said, there was a positive truth being stated, namely, that in all our traditional Christianity we have come to think of God far too much as a God concerned with religion rather than with the marketplace, with the world—a God concerned passionately with everything that is. Hence this radical attempt to de-religionize our concept of God.

The recovery came during the time of my ministry at Canterbury, and indeed it was incredible to behold.[4] I have always spent a lot of time visiting university campuses. There used to be a time when on any university campus, it seemed, one could not get a hearing unless one began with a political question. Only after that could one get back to God and the bearing of God on that particular question. Within a decade, however, the change was so great that young people were no longer asking to hear about political issues. Instead they were saying, "Talk to us about prayer. Talk to us about worship. Talk to us about contemplation, because unless you do so, we might want to go hear some guru." This was a quite startling change of emphasis, so much so that while one rejoiced in this return to religion, one also hoped it was not going to lead to a somewhat smug right-wing pietism.

A second conflict that is hitting Christians generally is that between a gospel of salvation through faith in Jesus, and a gospel concerned above all with the establishment of the kingdom of God. It is easy to caricature this tension—a gospel of salvation that exists in a social vacuum, on the one side, and the gospel of the kingdom of God that is only a political ideology masked as social justice. We Anglicans do not have a monopoly on the wisdom needed to solve that tension, but I think we have from our tradition something on which we can draw—namely, just that blending of social concern with the primacy of worship that we saw in William Temple.

Third, a more recent conflict concerns the uniqueness of the person of Christ and the historical certainty of the Gospel. Is it really possible to claim so much from a particular revelation in relation to the total action of God in the world He has made? Another aspect of this same question is the relationship between Christianity and the world religions. Now that world religions are getting to know one another better and appreciate one another more, is it possible for Christianity to continue its exclusive claim of there being but one Savior? Here again, we can draw upon a stock of Anglican wisdom that places a strong emphasis both on history and on experience. That means we can focus on a unique Savior while at the same time emphasizing the divine *logos* as the light that lightens everyone. Thus I believe that there is within our tradition something of real help for facing both the tensions among ourselves and the wider tensions in which all Christian traditions are involved.

There remains the question of our coherence as an Anglican Communion. The things that hold Anglicans together in the world are fewer than they used to be—a common stock of Anglo-Saxon culture helped keep our communion together, because the vast majority of Anglicans in the world spoke the English language. But the Anglican Communion has spread into so many continents and races that Anglo-Saxons are now a minority. Cultural bonds no longer operate as they once did. Anglicans also had the doctrinal bonds of the *Thirty-Nine Articles*. But the *Thirty-Nine Articles* have counted for less and less, and in all our Anglican churches they are regarded now as *venerated histori-cal documents* rather than as contemporary confessions. (Indeed in your American Prayer Book, you print the *Articles* so small I have to put on my glasses in order to read them!)

Liturgy, too, used to provide a very considerable bond—one prayer book used in Europe, England, America, Asia, Africa, anywhere—*that* prayer book no longer exists. And while there is some similarity amongst Anglican liturgies the world over, given, say, six specimens, I think you and I might be hard put to figure out which ones were Anglican and which were not.

A book by Professor Stephen Sykes called *The Integrity of Anglicanism*[5] complains quite rightly that Anglican integrity has been undermined by a kind of irresponsible pluralism. Anglicanism is being treated as a sort of intellectual club, in which, under the name of pluralism, any kind of doctrine is being taught and practiced. Sykes pleads for the integrity of Anglicanism, and I am entirely with him. I might define that integrity a little differently. He thinks in terms of a body of Anglican teaching, while I do not—for I do not think there is a distinctively Anglican doctrine of the Incarnation or of the Atonement. I think rather in terms of the Anglican *vocation*. The Anglican vocation and its appeal to God's revelation in Scripture and antiquity is embedded in our history and vital to our lives as Christians.

But if this Anglican vocation is to continue, then I think three things are necessary. First, we need a little more pride in some of the Anglican teachers. I hope to live to see in America the preoccupation with

Tillich to decline in such a way that some of the great Anglican teachers, including some of your own American Anglican teachers, may once more become familiar to you.

My second point is somewhat controversial. It does strain the unity of the Anglican Communion seriously when a particular Anglican Church veers off in some radical direction without the assurance of consensus, not caring or being cognizant always of the larger Anglican family. The two obvious issues are, of course, ordination and confirmation. It seems to me that a particular part of the Anglican Communion should not have made a total reevaluation of ordination and confirmation without a good deal of inter-Anglican consensus on the subjects. Please note what I am pleading for: not that the wisdom behind either is wrong, but that there should be more inter-Anglican consensus about those matters that are truly revolutionary in relation to Anglican union and witness in the world.[6]

My third point is this. To the spirit of theological education there is an Anglican shape—and one that is easy to describe and by no means difficult to practice. The Anglican shape of theological education simply means this: you study the Bible, and you study the ancient tradition, and you use your God-given reason in doing so. It is through the use of reason that we have a chance of making Scripture and tradition intelligible in the modern world. Theological education must not be a kind of menu in which you pick items here and there at random, but instead a shape where the necessity of Scripture and tradition and the modern use of reason in relation to it are integral parts. There is such a thing as Anglican theology and it is sorely needed in the present day.

The Theology of the Church

WE WILL NOW consider the Anglican approach to Christian unity in relationship to Rome, to the Holy Orthodox Church, and to the Protestant churches. Since the Anglican Communion claims to appeal to both Scripture and tradition, we need to look at these first for certain facts and principles that bear upon our understanding of the Holy Catholic Church and its unity.[1]

The New Testament writers use a variety of images for the church, among them the Body of Christ, the Temple, the Bride of Christ, and the True Vine. I want to emphasize another image that appears to me more basic than the rest because it goes back to the mission of Jesus and, indeed, behind the mission of Jesus to the Israel of God. This is the image of the People of God, the Israel of God, the *ecclesia*. When Jesus came proclaiming the kingdom of God, God's church already existed as the people Israel. The mission of Jesus was focused upon that nation in an attempt to convert Israel to accept the kingdom of God. "O Jerusalem, Jerusalem....How often would I have gathered your children together as a hen gathers her brood under her wings, and you would not. Behold, your house is forsaken and desolate "(Matt. 23:37-8).

Jesus, addressing the message of the kingdom of God to Israel and finding his message rejected, began to gather a remnant to be the nucleus of a newly constituted Israel. This nucleus was "the little flock" (Lk.

12:32) to whom Jesus promised the kingdom, and the core of it was the twelve. (The number twelve was, of course, symbolic, corresponding to the twelve tribes of Israel.) With this remnant Jesus made a divine covenant in his own blood. After his death, resurrection, and the coming of Pentecost the Christian community emerged as the new Israel, the new People of God, the new *ecclesia*.

In classical Greek the term *ecclesia* meant an assembly, a collection of people, like the assembly of the city of Athens, or the assembling of the ships in a fleet. But in the Greek Bible it signified the assembly of the congregation of the people of Israel and Israel as the divinely called community. Thus the great Christian claim that the baptized Christian community was itself God's Israel, and the Jews were, alas, by unbelief estranging themselves from God's true Israel. That belief lies behind the heartbreaking words of St. Paul in Romans 9-11. The Israel of God is one people, one *ecclesia*, and when St. Paul talks about the *ecclesia* of Corinth or Philippi, he means the one People of God as represented by the community in that particular place. This point is brought out very strongly in 1 Peter 2:9-10: "You are an elect race, a holy nation, a royal priesthood, a people for God's own possession." The New Testament writer has taken over the language Moses used in Exodus 19:6 about the People of God.

This idea has important implications for the church's unity. The church is basically a spiritual race and nation. Those who are baptized belong to this spiritual race and nation into which they have been reborn. The church's essential unity is one of kinship, and it means that our divisions are all the more scandalous because they are divisions within the family. The task then of unity is not the creation of unity, but finding those God-given structures and procedures that will give proper expression to this basic kinship of the new race, the People of God.

The People of God are described in a number of other images—the Body, the Vine, the Temple—expressing their intimate unity with the risen Christ, as a visible society to which you either belonged or did not belong. If you belonged you knew it, and other people knew it, too. The idea that God only knew who belonged to it seems deeply erroneous. God alone may have known who was going to be damned, ultimately, but God was not alone in knowing who belonged to the church and who did not. For the church has had from the beginning certain visible signs and marks that both proclaimed and manifested the grace of God, and also helped to define its own identity.

Baptism, for instance, proclaims the death and resurrection of Jesus that is the foundation of the church, and it is also *one baptism*, admission into *one body*—not Corinthian baptism or Antiochene baptism, but one baptism into one Body of Christ (Rom. 6:3; 1 Cor. 12:13). The Eucharist has the same twofold reference: it proclaims the Lord's death until the Lord returns. It is the means of the Christian's participation in the Lord's death, but it is also a symbol of the one Body of Christ everywhere: "We who many are one body, for we all partake of the one bread." (1 Cor. 10:17)

We have also the tradition of teaching, and the tradition of teaching has that same twofold aspect. It is teaching based on and derived from the Lord's death and resurrection. Jesus is Lord. Jesus, known to be crucified, is now alive. St. Paul describes his own basic teaching this way:

> For I handed on to you as of first importance what I in turn have received: that Christ died for our sins in accordance with the scriptures, and that he was buried, and that he was raised on the third day in

accordance with the scriptures, and that he appeared to Cephas, then to the twelve. (1 Cor. 15:3-5)

St. Paul teaches what he believes to be the basic teaching handed down to him, not what he thought it would be good for the people of Corinth to hear. We can be quite certain that it was substantially what he taught in every place. One tradition of teaching, no doubt very simple indeed in content, but applicable to all Christians everywhere as the teaching they must hear and respond to in order to be part of the one *ecclesia* of Christ.

We have the same double relationship with the ministry of the apostles, which is the other mark of the church.. The apostles have authority from Christ. They are witnesses to the resurrection of Christ, It was from there that the apostles derived their commission and their authority, but it was a ministry related to the whole church in its fullness. The apostle Paul reminds the Corinthians of teaching that belongs to him and to the whole church, and of behavior that belongs to the whole church as Christians. He reminds them that they are not the only Christians, that it was not to them alone that the Word of God came (1 Cor. 14:36). And in the simplest way possible, we can say that the apostolic ministry has this double reference to the foundation of Christ's authority through the resurrection, and the whole church in its fullness.

As the church moves into history, its simple life and its simple marks of identity and unity inevitably become complicated. There are the complications of becoming involved in the world's cultures, civilizations, and structures. There are the inevitable complications in the fuller drawing out of these basic facts and principles to serve the church in future times when the memories of the original events are growing dim, and the original generation is passing away. Thus the Eucharist becomes *liturgy*, comprehending the whole depth of the mystery of Christ in what is said and done. The tradition of teaching becomes more articulate, while the writings of the apostolic age are canonized and given authority as the witnesses to what the Lord Himself taught. This teaching is also summarized in baptismal creeds, becoming still more complex. So too the ministry of the apostles does not die out, but is succeeded by the historic episcopate, which is to fulfill the role the apostles once had in the church.

Here we do have to remind ourselves that the church is rather complex—a divine society, yet at the same time a growing institution amongst the world's institutions, composed of simple and fallible people. As one Anglican theologian writes, "We must face the tension between the institution that pays our salaries and the sacramental sign of Christ to the world. The disaster is to forget the tension and either to cling to the one to the exclusion of the other, or to identify the two superficially."[2] Those words point to the problem of the church in history and today. The church is the complex institution that organizes us, drives us hither and thither, sometimes pays us and sometimes does not. And the church is also Christ's own Body spiritually present in the world.

Let me suggest three principles about this tension that the New Testament writings themselves seem to suggest. First, we should always remember certain principles from the Old Testament. The church is God's people. It depends not on the faithfulness of its members, but on the faithfulness of the God who called it. When the church fails God through its own bad behavior, infidelity, and worldliness, the judgment of God falls upon it. The church can be for a time under the judgment of God. But God is always faithful, preserving the church and raising up a faithful remnant, from which may come a great spiritual renewal. The church is under a faithful God, a God both of wrath and of mercy, and that is why Jesus said to Simon Peter, "The gates of death shall not prevail against it" (Matt. 16:18).

The second principle is this. The church always lives in an eschatological context, already possessing wonderfully the unity, truth, and holiness Christ gave it throughout history's many ups and downs.[3] It is a pilgrim church as well as a possessing church. In St. Augustine's work *The City of God,* he contrasted the *ecclesia qualis nunc est* and the *ecclesia qualis tunc erit*—the church as she now is and the church as she will one day be.[4]

Think of some very simple biblical illustrations of this: "Now we are children of God. It doth not yet appear what we shall be...." (1 John 3:2) That surely applies to the life of the church as well as to Christians themselves. In Ephesians 4, the members of the church all grow together into the common apprehension of the truth and life that is in Christ, growing up into the full maturity of Christ. It may be something that happens in a few days; it may also be something that happens through *centuries*. The author of Ephesians 5 speaks of the Lord coming again to collect for himself a church without spot or wrinkle. If He came now, there would be spots and wrinkles, but one day He will come in the hope that those imperfections will be no more.

A third important consideration is the relationship between the church and the kingdom of God. The New Testament writings do not identify the church with the kingdom; the kingdom—*basileia*—means basically the sovereignty of God. This sovereignty is partly manifested in the community, and therefore in St. Matthew's gospel the term "the kingdom" is used a good deal for the community itself. Yet St. Matthew also teaches that the kingdom transcends the community; he includes much apocalyptic teaching about it. While this kingdom is partly realized in the Christian community the sovereignty of God transcends it. Identify the kingdom and the church completely and the result is the kind of ecclesiastical imperialism that has been such a curse in the history of western Christianity. If the distinction between the two is kept alive, we realize that the church is here to serve the kingdom, to promote its coming, to pray for its coming. Perhaps one day the church will be absorbed and identified with the kingdom; meanwhile it is the kingdom's servant and not the kingdom's possessor.

Let us now turn to see what early Christian tradition tells us about the church. We affirm over and over in the creed, "I believe in One, Holy, Catholic and Apostolic Church." What do we mean by that? We mean that while there can be many local churches, like a church of Philadelphia, a church of Corinth, a church of Chicago, or a church of Oconomowoc, there is but one Church of God. If there are two or three bodies all saying we are One, Holy, Catholic Church of Christ, either one of them is true and the rest are not, or else they all belong to it as the People of God and are making the mistake of claiming to be the *whole* People of God. But the oneness of the church is not only a numerical oneness, but the spiritual oneness of John 17, where Jesus prays that the disciples may be one through sharing in the oneness of the Father and the Son. It is the oneness of sharing in the divine life of the Blessed Trinity; it is a *qualitative oneness* that underlies the numerical oneness of the Holy Catholic Church.

This one church is holy as well because it is indwelt by the Holy Spirit, and Christians are called *hagioi*. That term is very striking. The Old Testament had referred to the whole people of Israel as the "holy people," but calling the members themselves *hagioi* emphasizes most powerfully that call to personal holiness belonging to the Christian as Christian. Yet while calling the Christians *hagioi*, the apostles were first to acknowledge the many, many blemishes in the church. The church is holy only through its possession of the Holy Spirit, and through the dedication of all its members to the way of holiness, reaffirmed again and again. Holiness is a continual and perhaps a lifelong process.

May I add here a cautionary note? While holiness is both a fact and a potentiality, it is impossible to enforce the holiness of the church by rejecting people who do not conform to certain moral canons. That has been tried often both in the history of the church, most notably by the early Puritans. When one says that the church is meant to be holy and therefore we will exclude those who are not holy, the inevitable happens. You can turn out the fornicators, the murderers, and those who apostasize in times of persecution; you can turn out sinners of every kind, but you can not turn out the sin of pride. This sin, the most deadly of all, is always present but not always easily identifiable. So if you are going to purge the church of sinners, you will need to purge it of the sin of pride and turn everybody out. As Anglicans, we believe that these attempts to purify the church by certain ethical criteria cause it to lose the reality of what it means to be dedicated to the holiness of God.

We now come to the Catholic aspect of the church. Unlike "One" and "Holy," "Catholic" is not a biblical term; it does not appear in the Greek Old Testament or New Testament. The term has come to mean something essentially whole, universal, instead of local or partial. Possibly the first appearance of the term in Christian literature is in St. Ignatius of Antioch in his address to the Smyrnaeans: "Wherever the bishop appears there let the people congregate; just as wherever Jesus Christ is, there is the Catholic Church."[5]

Wherever we find the grace-giving presence of Jesus Christ in the Christian community, there is the universal church. The church is as universal as the presence of Jesus Christ among the redeemed. The bishop does not define the presence of the church, but nonetheless the bishop is the one whose office represents this universality of the church, as distinct from a local church with local ministries.

Eventually this word "Catholic," or "universal," came to mean the authentic church as distinct from separate or irregular church bodies that were beginning to appear. The *Acts of Pionius*, one of the accounts of the trials of martyrs, for example, records that after the prisoner had testified that he was a Christian, the magistrate asked, "Of what church?" The martyr answered, "Of the Catholic Church." It suggests that by the time of this trial there were separatist churches that the magistrate might have heard of, and so he wanted to know which of these bodies the man belonged to.[6] An amusing instance of the same use of language is found in St. Cyril of Jerusalem's *Catechetical Lectures*. At one point, in giving advice to travelers, Cyril says, "When you are in a strange city, inquire for the Catholic church and not simply for the church, since heretics still call their meeting place by that name."[7] (That has a strangely modern ring—rather like our newspapers that have on every Saturday evening the announcement to attend the church of your choice!)

This same Cyril of Jerusalem also spoke of the meaning of Catholic in a way that goes far deeper, in language that is moving and glorious. Let me quote his wonderful description of what "Catholic" means in relation to the church:

> The Church is Catholic because she is throughout the whole world, from one end of the earth to the other; and because she teaches universally and without fail all the doctrines which ought to be brought to the knowledge of men concerning things visible and invisible in earth and heaven; and because she brings to the faith the whole of mankind, rulers and their subjects, educated and uneducated alike; and because she is a universal physician and healer of sins of every kind, sins of souls or of body, and possesses in herself every form of excellence that can be named, in deeds and words, and in spiritual gifts of every kind.[8]

I can think of nothing better than that Christian teaching should take that passage and make it the center of a great course of Christian education. What does it mean when you dare to call yourself a Catholic Christian? I belong to a church that reaches throughout the whole world; a church that teaches the whole of the truth about earth and about heaven; a church that addresses the same message to all alike, to the top people and the bottom people, the educated people and the uneducated people; a church that attempts to deal with the healing of all our infirmities, body and soul; a church that possesses all the virtues, all the fruits of the Spirit on which we can draw. As a Catholic Christian, I am pledged to all that. It is a marvelous, deep, and comprehensive picture.

Finally, there is the term "apostolic." We find it used in a variety of ways: founded by the apostles of Christ, being in continuity of life with the apostles of Christ, having that same mission from Christ the apostles had, maintaining the faith the apostles taught, and possessing a ministry and an authority in continuity with the apostles. The description of the church as apostolic, like Catholic, is deep and comprehensive, and not one to be used lightly, for no one aspect of it could ever exhaust the whole.

Within this talk of the church as apostolic, there is the special description of the historic episcopate as the apostolic succession. Since the phrase "apostolic succession" is often used clumsily and indiscriminately, it is important that we should bear in mind the three aspects of it that can be seen in early tradition, so that our use of the term may be discriminating instead of an unintelligent slogan.

The first aspect of apostolic succession to be emphasized in Christian literature was the continuity of bishop following bishop in their sees, which provided consistency of teaching. The bishops handed down from one to the other a primitive faith, and not what St. Irenaeus called the "fantasies of the Gnostics." In *Against the Heresies*, Irenaeus' *magnum opus* that made use of apostolic succession to combat Gnosticism, his main emphasis is not on the service of consecrating the bishop, but rather on the fact that there is continuity of teaching, because each bishop wanted to follow what his predecessor had taught.[9] (Of course the time might come when that might not be so, and we have to be warned against all manner of possibilities!)

A second aspect of apostolic succession is the bishops' performance of functions that the apostles performed; namely, preaching, ruling, and ordaining presbyters. The word "successors" (*diadochoi*) was applied to the bishops of the time by Hippolytus in the preamble to his work *Refutatio*. "The men who do the things that the apostles did" was how he explained it. The bishops do the things the apostles did. They are teachers, guardians of doctrine, chief shepherds of the people, and they ordain presbyters. Of course they can not do everything the apostles did, namely, be eyewitnesses to the Risen Jesus, and that is important to remember.

The third aspect of apostolic succession is what is sometimes called "the handing down of grace." Here we have to be very discriminating, because the phrase is crude and often clumsily used. All grace is the act of God in Christ. Anyone who is baptized or confirmed, consecrated a bishop or absolved—it is the gracious act of God in Christ. We need to get right away from the notion that grace is a kind of fluid that passes from the hands of the bishops onto an ordinand's head, who in turn passes it on. Language of that kind has been used, and we need at all cost to avoid it. Grace is the action of our Lord Jesus Christ, and a fresh action on every occasion.

In the tradition of the church, nonetheless, the functions of ordaining and consecrating bishops were confined to the latter, because by making the *bishop* the minister in this case, a special witness was borne to the church's unity and continuity. As the matter requires rather precise language to avoid errors of one kind or another, pray forgive me for quoting some words of my own:

> The succession of bishops is not an isolated channel of grace, since from the first Christ bestows grace through every sacramental act of His Body. But certain actions in this work of grace are confined to the bishops; and thereby the truth is taught that every local group or church depends upon the one life of the one Body, and that the church of any generation shares in the one historic society which is not past and dead but alive in the present. Thus the church's full and continuous life in grace does depend upon the succession of bishops, whose work, however, is not isolated but bound up with the whole Body.[10]

Heretical divisions came about in the early church that made these distinctions important. The Novatianists, for example, formed a separate body with strict moral views and excluded those who had lapsed under persecution. In his work *The Unity of the Catholic Church*, St. Cyprian argued that the Novatianists were simply outside the church, right outside, and their sacraments were not sacraments at all. Then a similar problem arose in connection with the Donatists, who separated themselves by taking an even more severe line about those who had lapsed under persecution. St. Augustine's response was that the Donatists, too, were outside the church, and it was this claim that so much frightened John Henry Newman many centuries later. Although the Donatists were outside the church, St. Augustine still held that their orders were valid because they were in the right "stream" of ordination. It may have been that view of Augustine's that helped beget a theory that orders had a validity apart from their place within the common life of the Body of Christ.

Another example is the Monophysites, a large body of eastern Christians who did not accept the Chalcedonian doctrine of Jesus' two natures. Monophysites believed the Incarnate Lord had one nature and they in fact minimized the humanity of Jesus, which brought about a major separation that has lasted to this day.

None of these divisions had a radical or distorting effect on Christendom as a whole. That was brought about by the separation of East and West, and the background to this separation is complex. The western church affirmed the universal jurisdiction of the Bishop of Rome in a manner that the eastern church could not accept, and tampered with the text of the Ecumenical Creed. On the other hand, the West objected to the East's stand on the veneration of icons, making it part of the tradition that defined the church's identity and continuity. This tragic situation was sealed in 1054 by the mutual anathematizing of the Bishops of Rome and Constantinople. Rome claimed that the East was outside the true church because it rejected the universal sovereignty of the Bishop of Rome, while Constantinople said the same thing about Rome because it did not conform to the fullness of its tradition. The consequences were so severe that both churches suffered grievously: the West lost the depth of eastern spirituality, while the East missed out on the West's intellectual activity. I think that all Christianity has suffered from this separation of the eastern and western churches.

In the final two lectures we shall discuss the Roman Catholic Church and Anglicanism's relationship to it, and we will also see how Anglicanism stands in relation to the Orthodox and Protestant churches. It is a terrible picture but also a glorious one. It is a terrible picture because these divisions contradict the purpose of the Lord and His church, but it is also a wonderful picture of the faithfulness of God—who does not forsake His church, but still goes on raising up saints to glorify Him.

Roman Catholicism and Anglicanism

THE ROMAN CATHOLIC Church had long claimed to be the One Holy Catholic Church of Christ in the world. Members of the Catholic Church, the Christian Church, were defined as those who are in communion with the See of Rome and accept the jurisdiction of the Pope. Indeed, the last century saw a considerable enhancement of what is called the "Ultramontane" position, for the Vatican Council of 1870 defined the infallibility of the Pope. Papal infallibility does not claim, as some people suppose, that every remark made by the Pope is infallible, but it does mean that when the Pope pronounces the collective decisions of the church, then what he says—under the guidance of the Holy Spirit—is infallible.

In fact, only a few pronouncements have ever been claimed to lie within the orbit of infallibility: the dogma of the Immaculate Conception of the Blessed Virgin, in 1854, the pronouncement of infallibility itself in 1870, and the dogma of the Assumption of the Blessed Virgin in 1950. Infallibility has been interpreted very diversely in the Roman Catholic Church. Some Roman Catholic theologians emphasize the corporate character of the church's decision-making in a council, and define infallibility as no more than the way the church makes an important decision, with the Pope merely announcing what that decision is. Yet the dogma of infallibility does appear to give the Pope an aura of infallibility, so that whatever he says has a way of being understood as statements to which the entire Roman Catholic Church is deeply committed.

Other actions have enhanced this separatist position. In 1897, Pope Leo XIII in a papal bull pronounced Anglican orders to be "null and void." Those whom the Anglican churches believe to be consecrated as bishops, or ordained as priests and deacons, do not possess those orders, and in the view of the Roman Catholic Church they are laity and nothing else.[1]

These intransigent notes were sounded into the Forties and Fifties, but in the Sixties there came about miraculous changes. The Second Vatican Council was summoned by Pope John XXIII, who died in the early part of it, and continued under the leadership of his successor, Pope Paul VI. Vatican II sat from 1962-65, and in its documents we find a new and different kind of spirit appearing in Roman Catholic theology. Some of them pertain to practical matters of church administration, while others deal with significant principles like ordination, the constitution of the church, the church's relationship to the contemporary world, and so on. The more important of these decrees are well worth reading because they present a certain unity, a fullness of view and presentation that is much closer to the Scriptures and the writers of the early church than to medieval scholasticism or the Council of Trent. Vatican II expressed a theological vision that is part liberal, part traditional and conservative, and with a unity of viewpoint from whose study all Christians can profit.[2]

For our purposes, the most important documents of Vatican II are those on revelation, on the nature of church, and on ecumenism.[3] Revelation is related to God's activity in the created world through the Word, summed up in the mystery of Christ: Christ the divine

Word made flesh, and Christ the new man in whom humanity is gathered into one and brought into union with himself. Scripture and tradition both witness to the mystery of Christ. The language used is largely biblical, and we are left with the feeling that the tradition is not merely an additional revelation, but a medium through which biblical revelation is presented.[4]

This sense of wholeness appears in the discussion of the Blessed Virgin Mary.[5] She is not a subject in herself, as no doubt earlier Roman Catholic thought would have made her. Instead she is treated within the context of the common life of the church on earth and in heaven, a common life in which the glory of the saints is a reflected glory of One who is Mary's own Son and Savior. I think students of the West and the East may appreciate that this treatment of the Virgin in relation to the church and the Communion of Saints is more characteristic of Eastern Orthodoxy than the western churches.

In this same document there is an awareness of the sadness of the division between East and West, a concern that is also rather new in Roman Catholic discussions. It was not surprising, therefore, that in the year after the Vatican Council closed, Pope Paul and Ecumenical Patriarch Athenagoras together made a declaration annulling the mutual anathema of 1054. That was a remarkable event characteristic of the underlying thought of the bishops at Vatican II.

In the Decree on the Church, the Vatican II discussion of ecclesiology places a striking emphasis upon the eschatological understanding of the church—the church as a pilgrim church. That emphasis, too, had not always been prominent in Roman Catholic thought. The church, which possesses from the beginning the treasure of ordination, is a pilgrim church. Indwelt by Christ who is the truth, the church still awaits the full measure of the meaning of that truth. Possessing unity by the Spirit, it is growing into the depth of unity in the Father and the Son. So we read in the Decree on the Church:

> The Church, to which we are all called in Christ Jesus, and in which we acquire sanctity through the grace of God, will attain her full perfection only in the glory of heaven....Until there is a new heaven and a new earth where justice dwells, the pilgrim Church in her sacraments and institutions, which pertain to this present time, takes on the appearance of this passing world. She herself dwells among creatures who groan and travail in pain until now and await the revelation of the sons of God.[6]

Now, that is very different from an ecclesiology that identifies the church in its present existence with the plenitude of God's kingdom. And it is within this thought about the church as a pilgrim that the language used is so striking. The church is said to be *semper reformanda* [7]—infallible yet always exposed to revelation, or, to put it better, always exposed to reformation in presenting the truth and holiness it possesses.

Here it is worth noticing that among other generous remarks about Christians separated from the Roman Catholic Church, Vatican II announces in this decree that such Christians may contribute something towards the sanctification and growth of Roman Catholicism. Perhaps these remarks are most remarkable of all: "Nor should we forget that whatever is wrought by the grace of the Holy Spirit in the hearts of our separated brethren can contribute to our own edification."[8] That is to say, Roman Catholics will not only tolerate the action of the Spirit in communities other than their own, but they will also expect that whatever the Holy Spirit does will help the edification of Roman Catholics themselves. That is wondrous.

One more theme of Vatican II I would mention concerns the church's looking beyond itself to the world, a world in which the divine *logos* is at work. Again, this is rich language. The world outside the Roman Catholic orbit is not just a mass of heathen from which nothing can be learned. No, the divine *logos* is at work in the sciences, which explore truth of many kinds, at work in men and women of goodness searching for justice and brotherhood, at work in the oppressed crying for deliverance, at work in the liturgies of other churches, whose fulfillment will one day come in Christ. The church faces a world in which the divine Spirit is at work:

> The joys and hopes, the griefs and anxieties of the people of this age, especially those who are poor or in any way afflicted, those too are the joys and hopes, the griefs and anxieties of Christ.....That is why this community realizes that it is truly and intimately linked with humanity and its history.[9]

And again, I quote:

> [In] the progress of the sciences, and the treasures hidden in the various forms of human culture, the nature of man himself is more clearly revealed and new roads to truth are opened....[Thus] a living exchange is fostered between the Church and the diverse cultures of people.[10]

This process of give and take, of teaching and learning, is possible because "the Church is 'the universal sacrament of salvation,' simultaneously manifesting and exercising the mystery of God's love for humanity."[11] Here is thinking we Anglicans learned from *Lux Mundi* just before the turn of the century, but have not heard from the Vatican until now.

Theological openness led to a new ecumenical attitude, too. Let me quote from the specific document, the "Decree on the Church," another document of Vatican II:

> The Church recognizes that in many ways she is linked with those who, being baptized, are honored with the name of Christian, though they do not profess the faith in its entirety or do not preserve unity of communion with the successor of Peter. For there are many who honor sacred Scripture, taking it as a norm of belief and of action, and who show a true religious zeal. They lovingly believe in God the Father Almighty and in Christ, Son of God and Savior. They are consecrated by baptism, through which they are united to Christ....Likewise, we can say that in some real way they are joined with us in the Holy Spirit, for to them also He gives His gifts and graces, and is thereby operative among them with His sanctifying power. Some indeed He has strengthened to the extent of the shedding of their blood.[12]

Furthermore,

> every renewal of the Church essentially consists in an increase of fidelity to her own calling. Undoubtedly this explains the dynamism of the movement toward unity. Christ summons the Church, as she goes her pilgrim way, to that continual reformation of which she always has need, insofar as she is an institution of people here on earth. Therefore, if the influence of events or of the times has led to deficiencies in conduct in Church discipline, or even in the formulation of doctrine...these should be appropriately rectified at the proper moment.[13]

This statement acknowledges, as I noted above, that Christians in their sanctified lives could help in the process of reformation.

There is one sentence in the Vatican II documents that deals specifically with Anglicanism. (Much is said, of course, about the Orthodox; while divergent in many ways, they do not present as many problems to Rome as the rest of us.) It reads: "Among those in which some Catholic traditions and institutions continue to exist, the Anglican Communion occupies a special place."[14] It is very significant that the sentence is there, and it is one to know and refer to often.

Since the Vatican Council closed, personal contacts and informal relationships have flourished between Roman Catholics and other Christians. It used to be impossible for these different groups to pray together, because even saying the "Our Father" together might have been understood as compromising their belief about God and the nature of the church. Praying together now is frequent; attending one anothers' churches is frequent; doing things together is frequent; recognizing one another as fellow Christians is frequent. It is fair to say that the atmosphere between Romans, Anglicans, and other Christians ready to respond to this crucial development has changed dramatically and miraculously.

In regard to relationships with the Anglican Communion, a key point was the meeting in March 1966 between Pope Paul VI and the Archbishop of Canterbury. What was said and done there had certain consequences. A Pope at Rome received an Archbishop of Canterbury as if he were the head of a Christian Communion. The Archbishop was received with these words, "We are happy to welcome you, not as strangers and sojourners but as fellow citizens with the Saints and members of the Household of God. Surely from heaven St. Gregory the Great and St. Augustine [of Canterbury] look down and bless." That is new language for Rome and Canterbury to speak to one another.[15] At the end of these meetings a "Common Declaration" was signed by each that spoke of a new atmosphere of Christian fellowship, calling upon the members of these two communities to treat one another with respect, esteem, and fraternal love. Then it went on to ask for dialogue between the communions on the theological questions that unite and divide us, as well as dialogue about some painful practical matters, such as the problem of mixed marriages.

But what was this dialogue to be based upon? Here is one phrase that I think will be remembered in history, for the basis of dialogue was to be "the Gospels and the ancient common Tradition." Not the Council of Trent or the theology of St. Thomas Aquinas, or the pronouncements of Vatican I, but "the Gospels and the ancient common Tradition."

Allow me to let you in on a secret here. Naturally there was a good deal of preliminary drafting and the exchanging of drafts before the actual day when the final document was ready, and people might have supposed that the phrase "the Gospels and the ancient common Tradition" was an Anglican suggestion, but it was not. Those were Pope Paul VI's own words, what he thought to be right, and he put those words into the draft himself.

As a consequence of that development, there came into existence the International Anglican-Roman Catholic Theological Commission, a body whose theologians came to represent a broad spectrum of Anglican churches and Roman Catholic theologians. Over the next few years this commission produced three reports on "Eucharist," "Ministry," and "Authority" with a very remarkable degree of agreement. As in Vatican II, they did not use scholastic terminology and concepts, but went back to biblical and patristic concepts.

The document on the Eucharist, for instance, spoke of Christ's being present in the Eucharist in a dynamic way, one that embodied what both Roman Catholics and Anglicans substantially believed. The document on ministry set the ordained priesthood and the episcopate in the context of the ministering priesthood of the whole church. The document on authority was a preliminary, rather than a finished statement, but it went quite a long way in discussing authority in terms of the church's collegiality, along lines that Vatican II had itself suggested.

These documents have no authority beyond that of the theologians who wrote them, but they do indicate that Roman Catholic and Anglican theologians are thinking in a way that, if it became widespread, could make agreement very possible indeed. In particular, no one doubts that if the line of thought in the document on ministry came to be accepted throughout the Church of Rome, it would completely cut the ground from under Pope Leo XIII, whose condemnation of Anglican orders would, I think, collapse out of sheer irrelevancy.

Other ecumenical developments took place in addition to the ARCIC documents. A joint commission on mixed marriages has produced very fruitful results, and the mandates from the Vatican about mixed marriages have been much more helpful than in the past. The way in which those mandates are interpreted tell us a good deal about how particular Roman Catholic hierarchies in different parts of the world are thinking. Some bishops have made no use of the new regulations whatever, while others have used them considerably, so that mixed marriages are free from the acrimony and pressures that used to accompany them.

Since Vatican II, however, not everything has proceeded along on these irenic lines. In both the Anglican Communion and the Roman Catholic Church there have been forces and movements that have run counter to Vatican II. We must understand that the Roman Catholic Church is a vast communion in which many, many winds are blowing, with Vatican II being only one of them. It is anyone's guess who is going to handle this problem, or who has the ear of the pope at any given moment. While there are factors within the Vatican wholly favorable to the Vatican II outlook and all its statements about ARCIC, there are also factors going the other way. I offer just this reflection: if we are troubled by the apparent diversity within the Anglican Communion and the frustrations it brings, I find it rather comforting to know that the Roman Catholic Church has about as much diversity and as many frustrations as we do.

So concerning the cause of unity, what inferences can we draw? Some say that if only there were more radicals in Rome and in the Anglican Communion, then radicalism might provide a basis for unity. I believe that view is wholly fallacious, because I think that mere radicalism cannot produce unity in the truth of Christ, but a watered-down version of Christianity. At the same time, there are those who think that if only the conservative factors in Rome and Anglicanism prevailed, then unity might result. I believe that to be equally fallacious, because conservatism in Rome means an "Ultramontane" position that does not recognize us at all, and conservatism in Anglicans may mean a position equally hostile to anything the Roman Church might do.

I am left with the conclusion that unity will not come from conservatism nor radicalism, but from the recovery in the Roman Communion of that kind of theological vision Vatican II saw: a vision that blends tradition and exploration. Equally, Anglicans need to recover a similar theological coherence, a recovery that is true to our own appeal to Scripture, tradition, and reason—an Anglican way that blends together the givenness of God's revelation and the exploration of its meaning in any age. I believe unity will come because the vision of Vatican II runs parallel to a good deal of the soundest Anglican vision both in the past and in the present, and it is the Lord's will that these two will come to understand one another and prevail.

Meanwhile the Anglican Communion is not a body seeking to be attached to the See of Rome. It has always looked in other directions as well, and enjoyed the closest of links with varieties of Protestant churches. In these links with Protestant churches, Anglicans have insisted on certain things—not a particular ideology, but simply what we believe to be basic Catholic facts and principles: the Scriptures, the sacraments of salvation (baptism and Eucharist), the creeds, and the apostolic ministry embodied in the historic episcopate. Given those basic facts and principles, Anglicans seem ready to be in communion with other Christians and create united churches with them. These efforts, alas, have involved a number of frustrations in different parts of the world, but also a number of real successes. In the Indian subcontinent, for example, Anglicans as such have disappeared into three united churches: the Church of South India, the Church of North India, and the Church of Pakistan. In each case, the Anglican approach to unity has not only included the facts and principles of the Lambeth Quadrilateral and the consecration of bishops in the apostolic succession, but also allowed elements of government and experience drawn from the other bodies.

Although the process of uniting with other church bodies was rapid a few years ago but is now slowing down, it has gone sufficiently far that there exist in the world a number of church bodies containing Anglicans and united with us on our principles. The three Indian churches I mentioned above are examples of that. All these churches together are called the "Wider Episcopal Fellowship."

It was evident from the beginning that if this movement of church unity were really successful, the Anglican Communion by that name might disappear. We have to face what that might involve. If the Anglican Communion disappeared because it was no longer fulfilling a mission, or abandoned its true mission, that would be sad indeed. But if the Anglican Communion were to disappear because of its good and great service in the reconciliation of all Christians, then its disappearance would be something in which we should rejoice. Why? Because in looking at the long term of God's purposes, we have to face this: the very term "Anglicanism" is one produced by the situation of sad Christian disunity, and the disappearance of Christian disunity might well mean the disappearance of the word "Anglicanism". Until that happens, we believe that God has given us real work to do, and "Anglicanism" describes that work. We are going to devote ourselves to our mission completely, not by viewing Anglicanism as an end in itself, but as a fragment of the One Holy Catholic Church of Christ.

The Orthodox Church and Anglicanism

THE SEPARATION OF eastern and western Christendom had two principal results. First, the Church of Rome made an exclusive claim to being the one church of God centered in the papacy. Second, the Church of the East, calling itself the Holy Orthodox Church, also claimed to be "The Christian Church," possessing identity and continuity with the church of Scripture, the Fathers, and the seven ecumenical councils.[1]

Let me put in a word here about terminology, because sometimes it can be confusing. The term "Oriental churches" is used to mean those that separated themselves from the main Catholic body after the Council of Chalcedon, rejecting Chalcedon because they were either Monophysite or Nestorian. These churches still exist in the Middle East and in Asia, though it is doubtful how much Monophysitism or Nestorianism still remains.

A second term is the "Uniate churches," or Eastern Rite Catholics. These are Eastern European churches that remain part of the Roman Communion; they are under the Pope's jurisdiction, but have eastern liturgies similar to those of the Orthodox. Roughly speaking, Eastern Rite Catholics are Catholics who dress and act like Orthodox. Of course their existence is rather resented by the Holy Orthodox Church, though they do play a reputable spiritual role.

The third phenomenon, and the one we are concerned with right now, is the Holy Orthodox Church. The Orthodox Church, while it has an inner spiritual unity and identity in liturgy and belief, is in fact made up of a group of churches—some of which are the ancient patriarchates of Constantinople, Jerusalem, Alexandria, and Antioch, and some of which are called "Autocephalous" churches. The latter have their own identity, like the Church of Greece or the Church of Yugoslavia, and do not have one of the ancient patriarchs at their head. While the Holy Orthodox Church exists primarily in Eastern Europe, Asia, and Northern Africa, it has come to have considerable membership in the West, and every one of the traditional Orthodox churches has its representatives here in the United States. I have always had the suspicion—which I hope is a fair one—that the Orthodox churches on this side of the Atlantic are perhaps less interested in their traditional spirituality than in their ethnic character, as Christian groups that profess loyalty both to ethnicity and the American way of life.

The Orthodox Church continues to be strong and powerful, and in Eastern Europe whole populations still profess allegiance to it. Here I merely want to indicate its theological and spiritual characteristics as distinct from western Christianity, whether Roman or Anglican or Protestant.

The first characteristic is its strong appeal to tradition, which it defines as the period of the seven ecumenical councils. That at once points to a difference, for while they have a devotion to the first four ecumenical councils, they have never been very interested in Councils Five, Six and Seven. We believe, you see, that Chalcedon settled matters decisively with regard to the doctrine of the Incarnation. Council Five is no more than a sort of addendum discussing some of the implications of Chalcedon; Council Six is about Monophysite issues that have become irrelevant in the West; while Council Seven deals with the veneration of icons, which is not a religious practice that has interested western Christians very much. By contrast the Holy Orthodox Church attaches great importance to its identity as a church in continuity with all the ecumenical councils.

Tradition is perhaps the most characteristic aspect of Orthodoxy. By tradition the Orthodox mean not just a body of teaching to supplement or elucidate the teachings of Scripture, but a whole stream of Christian life in the church. Tradition means the Scriptures, the doctrines, the creeds, the dogmas, and the whole life in the Spirit. It means the liturgies, the participation of the laity, the prayers of the faithful, the care of the children, the teaching, the Communion of the Saints—all that is part of what is called "holy tradition."

While the concept is very conservative indeed, it is not the conservatism of an institution or a dogmatic system so much as the conservatism of a totality of life, in which dogma and practical Christian life are of one piece. It is important to realize, therefore, that when Orthodox and non-Orthodox Christians talk about tradition, the term may be used in rather different ways.

Tradition in the Orthodox sense includes everything, and the "orthodox Orthodox" (if I may use such a paradoxical term) resent any suggestion that some things may be more important than others—the veneration of icons, the veneration of Mary, and the customs of the liturgy are all just as much parts of the tradition as the doctrine of the Incarnation. To understand, we have to think of it this way: tradition is one beautiful picture. It is God's own picture of what He has revealed for His family the church, and if there are any smudges on the picture anywhere, even small smudges, or if a little bit of the picture is cut out, then the whole picture is wrecked. That is why the Orthodox regard any deviation as a violation of that beautiful thing, the holy tradition God has revealed. It is a concept very different from ours, of course, but it ought to make us wonder whether our own ideas of tradition are wholly adequate.

Let us now consider the veneration of icons, which is a profound part of Orthodox personal and corporate piety and belief. In churches and at home one kisses and venerates the holy icons, and so bears witness symbolically to two truths. One is that the Creator manifests Himself through created objects, and we are affirming the sacramental principle of the universe when we venerate the icons. The other truth attests to the Communion of Saints, for by venerating the saints' pictures, we are venerating the saints themselves.[2]

When the Orthodox discuss icons with Anglicans, very often the discussion follows these lines. The Orthodox explain what they are doing; the Anglicans respond positively and say that is all very well and they, too, believe that the created order manifests God. Is the veneration of icons an absolutely vital way of bearing witness to that? Anglicans also value the Communion of Saints and join their prayers with the saints. Is the veneration of icons essential to that? To which the characteristic Orthodox answer would be, "Yes, the veneration of the icons is part of family life. It is the way the Christian family shows its belief, and so not to join in it is extraordinarily perverse." While the Orthodox view is very different from Anglicanism's more piecemeal approach, it constitutes a holistic understanding of faith, life, and tradition.

Believing as they do in the inviolability of the tradition of the seven councils and their identification with that tradition, the Orthodox resent greatly the papal claims and the western tradition relating to the *filioque* clause in the Nicene Creed. Probably that discussion is not so much about the metaphysics of the procession of the Holy Spirit as a discussion of the sinfulness of tampering with the original form of the Ecumenical Creed.

What about some practical characteristics of Orthodox spirituality? Here we are dealing with something that I think is not easy to define. The Orthodox and Anglicans believe in the resurrection of the Lord, but for the Orthodox, it is far more central to Christian life and worship than it is for Anglicans. While the West came to concentrate upon the commemoration of the Lord's death in liturgy and in life, and to think of Christianity as God manifesting Himself in the life of the world, the Orthodox tend to think of Christianity as God's lifting the world through Christ into the heavenly places, and of our worship as sharing in the actual liturgy of heaven. That is something you experience intensely in their liturgy, which can go on for hours, and you do not know when it starts or when it is going to stop because it represents the church on earth lifted for awhile into the timelessness of heaven's own worship.

This quotation from St. John Chrysostom embodies the idea that the Orthodox cling to so tenaciously:

> When thou seest the Lord sacrificed and lying as an oblation, and the priest standing by the sacrifice and praying, and all things reddened with that precious blood, dost thou think that thou art still among men, and still standing on earth? Nay, thou art straightway translated to heaven, so as to cast every carnal thought out of thy soul, and with un-

impeded soul and clean mind to behold the things
that are in heaven?[3]

The Orthodox also think about the Communion of
Saints in a way that is rather different from the West.
The Latin church wished to categorize and define the
afterlife. Souls in purgatory had to undergo a process
that was partly penal in character, and they badly
needed our prayers and masses and intercessions.
Beyond them was the realm of heaven in which Mary
and the saints dwell in glory, needing no prayers
themselves but exposed to our constant invocations
asking them to pray for us; they are so near the
throne of God that their intercessions must have tremendous power. In the eastern view, however, such a
dichotomy does not exist. There is one family that re-
flects the glory of God, and it includes the saints in
heaven, our own departed friends, and everyone else.
They are all one family, mixed together and reflecting
in different ways the glory of the one Christ.

The distinction, then, between "praying for" and
"praying to" disappears. The devout Orthodox will not
only pray *for* their dead friends, for the saints, and
even for the Blessed Virgin Mary, but they will also
pray *to* the Blessed Virgin Mary, the saints, and their
departed friends. The family unity of the Communion
of Saints cuts across these distinctions. Indeed the
glory of the transfigured Christ reflected in the saints
is a recurring Orthodox theme. The two great feasts of
Orthodoxy are the Epiphany and the Transfiguration,
and this fact in itself says a good deal about Orthodox
spirituality.

What about the ecumenical outreach of the Orthodox? Because of its strong belief in tradition, Orthodoxy is very exclusive—the one true church. Yet its
exclusivity does not take an institutional form—an institution to join and a set of dogmas to accept—but a

tradition and a life to share. The outlook towards non-Orthodox Christians is, rather, an invitation to come and share in the holy tradition. If the Anglican Communion really believed and practiced the tradition in its fullness, so the Orthodox argument goes, it would be part of the Holy Orthodox Church, and no more questions need be asked.

What, then, is the relationship of the Orthodox and the Anglican Communion? Ever since the Reformation Anglicans have been interested in the Orthodox as a church that, like itself, appeals to Scripture and antiquity, and is non-papal. The form of antiquity each appeals to is different, but nonetheless Anglicans have thought the Orthodox to belong to the same family as themselves. Yet although they frequently yearn to come together, centuries of separation have made the nuances of theological language so different that conversation is difficult. Pan-Anglican and pan-Orthodox dialogue is nearly impossible because the Orthodox churches, though they have a spiritual unity, are politically very separate. This is exacerbated by their modern political situation, for the rivalry between Moscow and Constantinople has been exploited by Soviet governments, which control the external movements of the Orthodox churches, thus making dialogue with western churches very difficult.

Nonetheless, in the Sixties and Seventies unofficial conversations, led by the Fellowship of St. Alban and St. Sergius, were followed by the first effort at pan-Anglican and pan-Orthodox dialogue. In 1962 the Ecumenical Patriarch and the Archbishop of Canterbury agreed to call for a joint theological commission to discuss the main matters of agreement and disagreement. Unfortunately the political difficulties made the process of keeping it together very slow indeed, but a few years of patience, when you are dealing with a separation of centuries, is something to be endured for the glory of God.

Between 1973 and 1976 the Joint Anglican-Orthodox Commission had several meetings, the first of their kind. *Anglican-Orthodox Dialogue* gives an outline of what had occurred in the past, leading to the climax in what is called the "Moscow Agreed Statement."[4] Published in 1976, it shows considerable understanding of the character of the differences, particularly on the meaning of tradition. The Orthodox show that the concept of timeless tradition is something we in the West might profit from learning about, and Anglicans show that tradition needs to be embodied in a historical world of process, history, and language to a greater extent than the Orthodox may realize.

To complete the story of the "Moscow Agreed Statement," the first Anglican-Orthodox dialogue for centuries took place at the same moment in 1976 that the Episcopal Church's General Convention voted to ordain women to the priesthood and episcopate. Is it surprising that the Orthodox were stunned, as well as those who had hoped a very long time for Anglican-Orthodox dialogue? The future, therefore, is in great uncertainty, and it would be very rash to prophesy about it because we are faced with a great number of unknowns. Perhaps it may not be God's providential plan that Anglicans are the people to bring together East and West; it may be for Rome and the East directly to do it. We simply do not know.

To end on this note of uncertainty, however, is not to end on a note of despair. We saw at the very beginning how the Anglicans of Richard Hooker's day valued knowlege highly, but still acknowledged that there are a good many things in God's purpose we cannot understand. Indeed, it has been the role of Anglicanism to criticize other Christian traditions that claim to know too much. The credibility of the church, not knowledge itself, is what matters most. The credibility of the church of God, and the credibility of Anglicanism, lies not in its own virtues or successes, but in the Lord of the church. And the Lord of the church is Jesus, crucified and risen, who through his church still converts sinners and creates saints.

Endnotes

Foreword: *A Portrait of Michael Ramsey*

1. Owen Chadwick, *Michael Ramsey: A Life* (Oxford: Oxford University Press, 1990), p. 76.

2. Bernard M.G. Reardon, *Religious Thought in the Victorian Age* (London: Longmans, 1980), p. 215.

The Anglican Spirit

1. A title conferred on Henry by Pope Leo X in 1521 in recognition of his book *Assertio Septum Sacramentum*, in which Henry defended the doctrine of the seven sacraments against Martin Luther. Henry's work was probably "ghosted" by Thomas More—see the excellent discussion in Richard Marius, *Thomas More* (New York: Knopf, 1984), pp. 276 ff.

2. The reference is to what has been amiably called the "Colloquy of Marbury" (1529), which left a deep estrangement between Luther and Zwingli. See Donald Ziegler, ed. *Great Debates of the Reformation* (New York: Random House, 1969), pp. 71-107.

3. Books I-VI were published in 1594 and V in 1597. Books VI and VIII appeared in 1648 and Book VII in 1662. I recommend the one-volume edition edited by A.S. McGrade and Brian Vickers, published in 1975 by St. Martin's Press.

4. Hooker, *Laws*, V, 67, XII.

Scripture, Antiquity, and Reason

1. Hooker, *Laws*, II, 8 VII.

2. White, *Treatise,* quoted in *Anglicanism*, ed. Paul Elmer More and Frank Leslie Cross (London: SPCK, 1957) pp. 8-9.

3. Lancelot Andrewes (1555-1626), Bishop of Winchester, wrote private prayers that were published after his death under the title *Preces Privatae* (1648).

4. The Cambridge Platonists flourished at Cambridge University between 1633-88, a group much influenced by the philosophies of Plato and Descartes. A solid study of them and their place and impact on Anglican theology is to be found in H. R. McAdoo, *The Spirit of Anglicanism* (New York: Scribners, 1965), pp. 81-155.

5. Benjamin Whichcote, *Several Discourses*, quoted in *Anglicanism*, p. 19. This was part of a sentence from a sermon preached by Whichcote on Philippians 3:12 entitled, "The Exercise and Progress of a Christian." The full sentence is, "The spirit in man is the candle of the Lord, lighted by God, and lighting men to God."

6. Joseph Butler (1692-1752) published *Analogy of Religion* in 1736, became Bishop of Bristol in 1738 and finally translated to Durham in 1750. It was at Bristol where Butler had his famous confrontations with both George Whitefield and John Wesley about evangelism. For a fine, stimulating essay on Butler's life see Herbert Hensley Henson's *Bishoprick Papers* (London: Oxford University Press, 1946), pp. 141-154.

Cultural and Political Anglicanism

1. Mark Pattison, *Essays* (Oxford, 1889), p. 267.

2. George Herbert, "The British Church" in *The Works of George Herbert* (London: Oxford University Press, 1970), p. 109.

3. John Bunyan (1628-88), an Independent preacher who was jailed from 1660-72 and published *Pilgrim's Progress* in two parts, 1678 and 1684. Richard Baxter (1615-91) Puritan clergyman, wrote *The Reformed Pastor* in 1656. He also

wrote several hymns including "Ye Holy Angels Bright". Isaac Watts (1674-1748) Independent pastor, is justly acclaimed as one of the greatest of English hymn writers and the author of "Jesus Shall Reign Where'er the Sun" and "O God, Our Help in Ages Past".

4. John Wesley (1703-1791) and his brother Charles (1707-1781) were the founders of Methodism. It must be said in all fairness that Charles Wesley never left the Church of England, while his brother claimed on his deathbed not to have done so. For a superb discussion and exposition of Charles Wesley's eucharistic hymns, see Geoffrey Wainwright, *Eucharist and Eschatology* (New York: Oxford University Press, 1981). William Bright (1824-1901) was a church historian and hymn writer who composed the eucharistic hymn, "And Now O Father, Mindful of the Love". John Mason Neale (1813-1866) was a prolific hymn writer, translator of Greek and Latin hymns, and author of children's books.

5. John Smith, "Advertisement for the Unexperienced Planters of New England", quoted in Charles Tiffany, *A History of the Protestant Episcopal Church in the U.S.A.* (New York: Christian Literature Company, 1895), p. 13.

6. Samuel Seabury (1729-96) was the first bishop of the Episcopal Church in America. See the account of his ordination in its historical context in Frederick V. Mills, *Bishops by Ballot* (New York: Oxford University Press, 1978).

7. John Henry Newman, *British Critic*, vol. 26, p. 281, and Henry Liddon, *Life of E. B. Pusey*, vol. 3, p. 349.

Anglo-Catholicism and the Oxford Movement

1. Thomas Arnold (1795-1842) was appointed Headmaster of Rugby in 1828, and Regius Professor of Modern History at Oxford in 1841.

2. Arthur Penryn Stanley (1815-81) was educated at Rugby under Thomas Arnold and was Dean of Westminster from 1864 till his death.

3. Owen Chadwick remarks in *The Victorian Church* that *The Christian Year* was so well known that even in the 1860's or 70's, if a person had quoted some lines to a group of churchmen, two or three of them could have finished the stanza.

4. John Henry Newman (1801-90) is to many the most attractive of the Tractarians. In addition to the standard biographies of him by W. Ward (1912) and Muriel Trevor (1962), I recommend Geoffrey Faber's dazzling *Oxford Apostles* (1933), J.M. Cameron's stimulating articles on Newman, especially his *John Henry Newman* published by the British Council in 1956, Owen Chadwick's *Newman* (1983), and the extremely fine biography by Ian Ker, *John Henry Newman* (London and New York: Oxford University Press, 1988). Finally, Newman's own *Apologia pro vita sua* (1864) should not be neglected, although it is a self-defense and therefore highly selective.

5. Newman's *Parochial and Plain Sermons* were published in eight volumes in 1868.

6. *Ibid.*, 4:179ff.

7. *Ibid.*, 5:10-11.

8. Pusey wrote Tract Sixty-Seven, *Scriptural Views of Holy Baptism* in 1836. He continued to write the next two tracts on baptism also, so that taken together they make a full-length treatise. Incidentally, it was just this fuller development of the Tractarian views that frightened away some earlier sympathizers.

9. Keble's *On Eucharistical Adoration* was published in 1857. Pusey's sermon was preached before the University in 1843 and was so controversial that he was suspended from preaching at the University for two years. The other prominent Tractarian work on the Holy Eucharist was Robert Wilberforce's *The Doctrine of the Incarnation* (1848).

10. Ramsey notes that Pusey's sermon "Entire Absolution of the Penitent", preached in 1846, should be consulted. This

sermon was a part of a series Pusey had planned in 1843, a course entitled, "Comforts to the Penitent."

11. John Henry Newman, *Lectures on Justification* (1838), pp. 336-7.

12. See David L. Edwards' excellent discussion of this incident in his *Leaders of the Church of England 1828-1944* (London: Oxford University Press, 1971), pp. 6ff. Edwards' entire essay on Newman is one of the most satisfying to be found.

13. *Ibid.*, p. 67.

14. Newman's *An Essay on the Development of Christian Doctrine* (1845) was reissued by Penguin Books in 1974 with a beautifully written introduction by the editor, J.M. Cameron.

After the Tractarians

1. The Society of St. John the Evangelist was founded by Richard Benson (1824-1915), Vicar of St. James, Cowley from 1850 on. Its primary emphasis was the life of prayer under monastic vows, but was also involved in missionary and educational efforts. For a history of the Anglican religious revival, including the Cowley Fathers, see A.M. Allchin, *The Silent Rebellion*, (London: SCM, 1958). See also Martin Smith, ed., *Benson of Cowley* (Cambridge, MA: Cowley, 1982).

2. Ordained in 1856, Charles Grafton (1830-1912) was much influenced by Pusey. He was rector of Church of the Ascension in Boston from 1872-1888 before becoming Bishop of Fond du Lac, and known for his holiness and ecumenism.

3. Pusey's sermon was preached in 1878, twenty years after Darwin's *Origin of the Species*. For a highly readable account of the conflict between Victorian Christianity and science, see William Irvine's *Apes, Angels, and Victorians* (New York: McGraw-Hill, 1955).

4. Charles Grafton, *A Journey Godward* (New York: Longmans, Green, and Co., 1914), pp. 183-4.

5. See A.M. Ramsey, *The Gospel and the Catholic Church* (Cambridge, MA: Cowley, 1989), pp. 68-85.

6. See *The Life of Frederick Denison Maurice, Chiefly Told in His Own Letters* (New York: Charles Scribner, 1884), edited by his son Frederick in two volumes, and hereafter cited as *Life*. The best introductions to Maurice are found in A.M. Ramsey, *F.D. Maurice and the Conflicts of Modern Theology* (Cambridge: Cambridge University Press, 1951); A.R. Vidler, *Witness to the Light* (New York: Charles Scribner, 1948), published in England under the title *The Theology of F. D. Maurice*; Olive Brose, *Rebellious Conformist* (Gambier, OH: Ohio University Press, 1971). Additionally, the excellent profile of Maurice in Edwards' *Leaders of the Church of England*, pp. 134-156, should not be missed.

7. *Life* 1:225-6.

8. *Life* 2:359.

9. *Life* 1:369.

10. Maurice's views were published in his *Theological Essays* (London, 1853). For a full discussion of the conflict which led to Maurice being expelled from King's College, London, see *Life* 2:163-209. Ramsey's own detailed comments are found in his F.D. Maurice and the Conflicts of Modern Theology, pp. 48-54.

11. *Life* 2:35. (Emphasis added.)

12. *Life* 2:494.

13. Quoted from Ramsey, *F.D. Maurice*, p. 55.

14. Samuel Rolles Driver (1846-1914) succeeded Pusey to the Regis Professorship of Hebrew at Oxford and Canon of Christ Church. His *Introduction to the Literature of the Old Testament* (1897) remained the standard work for some fifty years. Joseph Barber Lightfoot (1828-89) taught New Testament studies and theology at Cambridge. Brooke Foss Westcott (1825-1901) collaborated with F.J.A. Hort on the critical

Greek text of the New Testament. Fenton John Anthony Hort (1828-92) also taught at Trinity, Cambridge after 1872. For a fine survey of the rise of the higher criticism of the New Testament in England and elsewhere, see Stephen Neill, *The Interpretation of the New Testament 1861-1961* (London: Oxford University Press, 1964).

15. F.J. A. Hort, *The Way the Truth the Life*, published posthumously in 1893, was originally his Hulsean Lectures for 1871; see p. 75.

Charles Gore and Liberal Catholicism

1. Phillips Brooks (1835-93) become rector of Holy Trinity, Boston in 1869 and Bishop of Massachusetts in 1891, He was a remarkably gifted, evangelical preacher with an acute social conscience, whose piety is evident in his hymn, "O Little Town of Bethlehem."

2. Brooks's *Lectures on Preaching* (1877) express his view that preaching is the proclamation of truth through personality.

3. William Porcher DuBose (1836-1918) is considered to be the most original and creative thinker yet produced by the American Episcopal Church. Next to the book mentioned below, his best known work was *The Soteriology of the New Testament* (1897). For a fine introduction to his thought, see Jon Alexander, O.P., *William Porcher Dubose* (New York: Paulist Press, 1988).

4. William Porcher DuBose, *The Gospel in the Gospels* (London: Longman's, 1906), pp. 272f.

5. *Ibid.* p. 274.

6. *Lux Mundi* was published in 1889 by John Murray. The authors were Henry Scott Holland, Aubrey Moore, J.R. Illingworth, R.C. Moberly, Arthur Lyttleton, Charles Gore, Walter Lock, Francis Paget, W.J.H. Campion, and Robert Ottley.

7. For a full discussion of *Lux Mundi* and liberal Catholi-cism, see Ramsey's survey, *From Gore to Temple* (London: Longman's 1960), published in the United States as *An Era in Anglican Theology*. Biographies of Charles Gore include G.L. Prestige, *The Life of Charles Gore: A Great Englishman* (Heinemann, 1935) and James Carpenter, *Gore: A Study in Liberal Catholic Thought* (Faith Press, 1960).

8. Aubrey Moore, "The Christian Doctrine of God" in *Lux Mundi*, p. 99.

9. For a more detailed discussion of Gore's views of the In-carnation, see *From Gore to Temple*, pp. 16-29.

10. *Ibid.*, pp. 5-6, 30-43.

11. *Lux Mundi*, p. 360, in the first and second editions.

12. In November of 1917, the Prime Minister Lloyd George made his first episcopal nomination, Hensley Henson to the See of Hereford. Because of Henson's frequent provocative writings on the articles of the creed that revealed an agnos-tic approach to the virgin birth and the bodily resurrection of Jesus, Bishop Gore was among those who protested the nom-ination. See *From Gore to Temple*, pp. 83ff.

William Temple

1. Frederick Temple (1821-1902) was a remarkable man who became Bishop of Exeter in 1869 and subsequently Bishop of London and Archbishop of Canterbury. He was known for his working class origins, his promotion of the temperance movement, and his warm earnest preaching. See Edwards, *Leaders of the Church of England*, pp. 286-332.

2. William Temple, *The Church Looks Forward* (New York: Macmillan, 1944), p. 19. The original quotation was: "People are always thinking that conduct is supremely important, and that because prayer helps it, therefore prayer is good. That is true as far as it goes; still truer is it to say that wor-ship is of supreme importance and conduct tests it. Conduct

tests how much of yourself was in the worship you gave to God."

3. Ramsey is alluding to a preparatory meeting of the Oxford Conference held in 1936 at Bishopthorpe. At the age of thirty-two Ramsey had just published *The Gospel and the Catholic Church*, which brought him to Temple's attention.

4. William Temple, *Nature, Man and God* (London: Macmillan, 1934); *Christus Veritas* (London: Macmillan, 1924); *Readings in St. John's Gospel*, 2 vols (London: Macmillan, 1939-1940).

5. The reference is to Jurgen Moltmann, German theologian and author of the seminal *Theology of Hope* (New York: Harper and Row, 1967).

6. *Christus Veritas*, p. 270.

7. *Ibid.*, p. 269.

8. *Ibid.*, p. 269.

9. Compare *Nature, Man and God*, pp. 306-7.

10. See William Temple, "Revelation" in *Revelation: A Symposium*, John Baillie and Hugh Martin, eds. (London: Faber and Faber, 1937), p. 107.

11. Temple's fullest discussion of economics and the social order is found in his *Christianity and the Social Order* (New York: Penguin Books, 1942).

12. Temple's sermon, preached in 1932, included the sentence: "We have to ask not only who dropped the match, but who strewed the ground with gunpowder". Quoted in F. A. Iremonger, *William Temple, His Life and Letters* (London: Oxford University Press, 1948), p. 376.

13. See Iremonger, pp. 540-68.

14. See William Temple, *Ethics of Penal Action* (London: National Association of Probation Officers, 1934) and *Ethics of Punishment* (London: Howard League for Penal Reform, 1945). See also Iremonger, pp. 443-5. Bishop Ramsey's maiden speech in the House of Lords, given 9 July 1956,

strongly opposed capital punishment. As Archbishop of Canterbury, he helped lead the fight to pass the Abolition of Death Penalty Bill by his speech in the House of Lords on 20 July 1965. This speech was published in Ramsey's *Canterbury Pilgrim*, pp. 139-143.

15. In addition to Iremonger's biography mentioned above, for more on William Temple's life see Joseph Fletcher, *William Temple: Twentieth Century Christian* (New York: Seabury Press, 1963).

16. Chairman's Introduction in *Doctrine in the Church of England* (London: Macmillan, 1938).

17. Quoted in *From Gore to Temple*, p. 160.

18. *Ibid.*, pp. 161-2.

19. *Ibid.*, p. 162.

Biblical Theology and Christian Renewal

1. The "Faith and Order" movement was begun earlier in this century to bring about reunion of the Christian churches. The "Life and Work" movement focused on the relation of Christianity to society, politics, and economics, and in 1948 the two movements merged into the World Council of Churches. Temple and George Bell were prominent among Anglicans in the arduous work of preparing for the WCC. George Bell (1881-1958) became Bishop of Chichester in 1929 and was primarily known for his ecumenical work. During the Second World War his outspoken criticism of the indiscriminate bombing of Germany may have cost him the opportunity of going to Canterbury in 1944. See Ronald C.D. Jasper, *George Bell, Bishop of Chichester* (London: Oxford University Press, 1967).

2. Edwyn Clement Hoskyns (1884-1937) was Dean of Chapel of Corpus Christi College, Cambridge from 1919 till his death, and the foremost Anglican New Testament scholar of his day. Hoskyns was Ramsey's teacher at Cambridge in the 1920s.

3. Gerhard Kittel's *Theological Dictionary of the New Testament*, in nine volumes, was published between 1933 and 1973.

4. See Bishop Ramsey's detailed evaluation of the "Death of God" movement and other theological tendencies of the Sixties in his *God, Christ, and the World* (London: SCM, 1969).

5. Stephen W. Sykes, *The Integrity of Anglicanism* (New York: Seabury Press, 1978).

6. There is no better discussion of the issues raised by Ramsey here than the closely reasoned essay by Paul Avis entitled *Anglicanism and the Christian Church* (Minneapolis, MN: Augsburg Fortress, 1989).

The Theology of the Church

1. This chapter on the theology of the church is a good overview of Ramsey's first book, *The Gospel and the Catholic Church*, published over fifty years ago.

2. James E. Griffiss, "Preliminary Material on the Doctrine of the Church and Sacraments" (unpublished manuscript), p. 1 (Nashotah House Library).

3. See Ramsey's extended comments on the theme in his address to the World Council of Churches in 1961 in *Canterbury Essays and Addresses* (London: SPCK, 1964), pp. 55-9, and his more updated understanding in his sermon to the bishops of Lambeth Conference in J. B. Simpson and E. M. Story, *The Long Shadows of Lambeth X* (New York: McGraw-Hill, 1969), pp. 286-7.

4. Augustine, *City of God*, 10:9.

5. Ignatius, *Epistle to the Smyrnaeans*, 8.

6. *Acts of Pionius*, 16:5.

7. Cyril of Jerusalem, *Catechetical Lectures*, 18:26.

8. *Ibid.*, 13:23.

9. Irenaeus, *Against Heresy*, 3:3:6.

10. Ramsey, *The Gospel and the Catholic Church*, pp. 82-3.

Roman Catholicism and Anglicanism

1. See the fine history of this event by John Jay Hughes, *Absolutely Null and Utterly Void* (New York: Sheed and Ward, 1968).

2. I have found that the most accessible publication of the decrees and documents of Vatican II is that edited by Walter M. Abbott, S.J., *The Documents of Vatican II* (New York: The American Press, 1966).

3. The official titles for the decrees are: "Dogmatic Constitution on Divine Revelation" (*Dei Verbum*); "Dogmatic Constitution on the Church" (*Lumen Gentium*); "Pastoral Constitution on the Church in the Modern World" (*Gaudiam et Spes*); and "Decree on Ecumenism" (*Unitatis Redintegratio*).

4. Cf. "Dogmatic Constitution on Divine Revelation", pp. 111-128.

5. Cf. "On the Church", pp. 85-96.

6. "On the Church", pp. 78,79.

7. "Ecumenism", p. 350.

8. "Ecumenism", p. 349.

9. "Ecumenism", p. 349.

10. "Pastoral Constitution on the Church in the Modern World", pp. 199-200.

11. "Pastoral", p. 246.

12. "Pastoral" p. 247.

13. "On the Church", pp. 33-4.

14. "Decree on Ecumenism", p. 350.

15. "Ecumenism", p. 356.

16. See the study on the relationship of the Roman and Anglican Communions by Bernard and Margaret Pawley entitled *Rome and Canterbury: Through Four Centuries* (New York: Seabury Press, 1975). The meetings of Archbishop Ramsey and Pope Paul VI are described on pages 352-62.

The Orthodox Church and Anglicanism

1. There has been a rapidly growing body of literature on the Eastern Orthodox Churches since the mid 1960's. See the very fine introductions by Kallistos Ware in *The Orthodox Church* (Baltimore: Penguin Books, 1959), and *The Orthodox Way* (London: SPCK, 1979). On the doctrinal history of the Eastern Churches, see Jaroslav Pelikan's *The Spirit of Eastern Christendom* (Chicago: University of Chicago Press, 1975). A.M. Allchin wrote about Bishop Ramsey's devotion to the cause of Christian unity, and particularly his great foresight and sensitivity in reaching out to the Eastern Orthodox in "Approaches to Eastern Orthodoxy and Rome", in *The Great Christian Centuries to Come: Essays in honor of A.M. Ramsey* (London: Mowbray, 1974). Finally, I am happy to commend the book by my friend and fellow Nashotah House student of Ramsey, E.C. Miller, Jr., *Toward a Fuller Vision: Orthodoxy and the Anglican Experience* (Wilton, CT: Morehouse Barlow, 1984). The last chapter entitled "Orthodoxy and the theology of Michael Ramsey", is a very moving tribute to one whom Miller considers above all an ecumenical theologian.

2. See Michael Ramsey, "The Communion of Saints", in "Sobornost" (1981)3:2:192-196.

3. St. John Chrysostom, *On the Sacred*, 3:4.

4. Kallistos Ware and Colin Davey, ed., *Anglican-Orthodox Dialogue: The Moscow Agreed Statement* (London: SPCK, 1977).

5. Bishop Ramsey's despair was partially turned to joy when the Orthodox decided to continue meeting with the Anglicans and produced a further statement concerning various agreements as described in *Anglican-Orthodox Dialogue: The Dublin Agreed Statement 1984* (London: St. Vladimir's Seminary Press, 1985).

Index

Bell, George K.A. 108

Benson, Richard Meux 65

Bible. *See* Scripture, Holy

Biblical theology 108 - 110

Bishops. *See* Episcopate

Bonhoeffer, Dietrich 110

Book of Common Prayer 16 -
   18, 35, 39, 43 - 44, 114
   1549 Edition 13 - 14, 16
   1552 Edition14, 16

Booth, William 4

Bright, William 40

Broad Church 55. *See also*
   Latitudinarianism

Brooks, Phillips 81

Brunner, Emil 97

Bultmann, Rudolf 109 - 110

Bunyan, John 39

Butler, Joseph 3, 6 - 7, 31

C

Calvin, John 14, 17, 22
   Calvinism 14, 17, 19, 22, 27 -
   28
   and predestination 17, 22, 27

Cappadocian Fathers 90

Cambridge Platonists 31

Caroline Divines 18, 50

Catholicity 12, 15 -16, 26, 38,
   40 - 41, 45, 50, 52 -53, 63,
   67 - 68, 117, 123 - 127, 141 -
   142

Chadwick, Owen 3

Chalcedon, Council of 63,
   129, 143 - 145

Charismatics 7 - 8

Charles I, King 38

Charles II, King 38 - 39, 44

Chartists 75

Christian Socialism 1, 70, 74
   - 76.

Chrysostom, John 30, 147

Church, doctrine of. *See* Apostolic succession; Baptism,
   Holy; Catholicity; Episcopate; Eschatology; Eu-
   charist, Holy; Holiness of
   the church; Kingdom of
   God; Ministry; National
   church, idea of; Reason;
   Roman Catholicism; Royal
   supremacy; Sacraments;
   Scripture, Holy; Tradition;
   Unity of the church; Worship

Church Fathers 26 - 27, 29,
   33, 50 - 51, 55, 63, 66, 90,
   95, 101, 143

Church of England 1, 4 - 5, 8,
   12, 16, 26, 37, 40 - 42, 49 -
   50, 52, 54, 97

Church of North India 141 -
   142

Church of Pakistan 141 - 142

Church of South India 141 -
   142

Communion. *See* Eucharist,
   Holy

Communion of Saints. *See*
   Saints, Communion of

Pusey, Edward Bouverie 41, 45, 51 - 52, 54, 56, 58, 66

Q

Quick, O.C. 87

R

Ramsey, Frank P. 2 - 3

Real Presence. *See* Eucharist, Holy

Reardon, Bernard M.G. 4

Reason 115
Anglican appeal to 21, 23, 30 - 35, 90, 108, 115, 140

Reformation 13 - 14, 17, 29, 149

Redemption, doctrine of 17, 72. *See also* Atonement; Justification, doctrine of; Salvation

Revelation, divine 11, 19, 21, 24 - 25, 30 - 33, 67, 69 - 70, 72 - 73, 77 - 79, 83, 85 - 87, 90, 97, 100 - 102, 109, 113 - 114, 132 - 134, 141

Robinson, John A.T. 4

Roman Catholicism 13 - 14, 17, 19, 23, 37, 40, 58, 61 - 63, 89, 109, 131 - 35, 137 - 40, 143 - 44. *See also* Papacy; Trent, council of; Vatican councils
and Anglicanism 130, 132, 137 - 41
doctrine in 89 - 90
ecclesiology of 133 - 35

and ecumenism 117, 132 - 137
Ultramontanism in 131, 140
Uniate churches 143
and the Virgin Mary 131, 133

Royal supremacy 12 - 13, 15 - 16, 38, 41 - 42, 46

Runcie, Robert 9

Russell, Bertrand 3

S

Sacraments 15 - 16, 18, 24, 53, 55, 61, 111, 129, 134, 141. *See also* Baptism, Holy; Confirmation, sacrament of; Eucharist, Holy; Penance, sacrament of

Saints, Communion of 29 - 30, 53, 133, 145 - 46, 148
veneration of 61, 146

Sanctification, doctrine of 57 - 58

Salvation 17, 23 - 26, 32 - 33, 62, 72, 74, 77, 83, 104, 112 - 113. *See also* Atonement; Justification, doctrine of

Scientific revolution 32, 49, 65 - 66, 69, 77 - 78

Scripture, Holy 13, 15, 24 - 26, 29, 32 - 34, 65, 67, 77, 86, 95, 97, 101, 108 - 10, 113, 115, 119 - 21, 132 - 33, 136, 143, 145, 149
Anglican view of 22 - 28, 33 - 35, 90, 108, 111, 114 - 15, 117, 140 - 41
and biblical criticism 32, 65, 77 - 78, 86 - 87, 108 - 09
and the church 69
literalistic interpretations of 32 - 34, 66, 86, 90, 108 - 09

COWLEY PUBLICATIONS IS a ministry of the Society of St. John the Evangelist, a religious community for men in the Episcopal Church. Emerging from the Society's tradition of prayer, theological reflection, and diversity of mission, the press is centered in the rich heritage of the Anglican Communion.

Cowley Publications seeks to provide books, audio cassettes, and other resources for the ongoing theological exploration and spiritual development of the Episcopal Church and others in the body of Christ. To this end, it is dedicated to developing a new generation of theological writers, encouraging them to produce timely, creative, and stimulating publications of excellence, and making these publications available widely, reaching both clergy and lay persons.